AND
THEN
THERE
WAS
HEAVEN

Roland M. Comtois

CHALICE
COMMUNICATIONS

Published by Chalice Communications
East Killingly, Connecticut
www.chalicecommunications.com

Copyright © 2009 by Roland M. Comtois
www.rolandcomtois.net

Cover design by Bob Callahan
Book design by Bob Callahan
Editorial by Cindy Clarke

Printed in the United States of America

First Printing: May 2009
Second Printing: May 2011

ISBN: 978-0-9824536-0-5

ACKNOWLEDGEMENTS

To GOD, my Angels, Guides and Guardians, Masters and Teachers...my faithfulness is absolute.

To every person who has whispered a word of encouragement and offered unconditional love...I thank you from my heart to yours for your generosity.

In life, every being touches another and in some way those listed here have shaped my destiny, for that I am grateful:

To Cindy Clarke, this book would have remained a vision quietly tucked away in some distant place without you. I cannot thank you enough for your belief in my story and for your creativity and talent, in making *And Then There Was Heaven* a reality.

To Beverly Russo-Lussier and my cousin Debbie Grenon, your love and support from the very beginning is immeasurable. Thank you for taking this journey with me and especially for the 7 PM phone calls when channeled messages needed to be shared.

To my friend, teacher and spiritual mother, the late Reverend Tullia Forlani Kidde, I am forever indebted for your love and your steadfast belief in me. Thanks for holding my manuscript and believing in its truth. Our souls are bound by divine love.

To my dear, dear friends when I needed the validation you were there, when I needed hope you were there, when I needed an angel, you were sent; JoAnn Wolff, Patricia Pepler, Linda Hogan, Eleanor Bently, Normand Rene' Poulin, Joanne Bartholomy, Barb Conetta, Mary Muryn, Susan L. Arel-Comtois, Suzanne Robidoux, Shelley Boyer, Jerilyn DesGranges, Chip and Nancy Cingari, Helen Celestine Escoffier, my godmother Pauline Jette, Frank and Louise Aridano, Kathy St. Germain, Linda Love, Wayne Foster, Lori A. Denomme, Joseph M. Loffredo and all of my wonderful friends at Friendly Home.

To Bob Callahan, your ability to see that which lies deeply within the pages of my book is divine, and your creation is heavenly.

To my Mom, Theresa Comtois, your life has truly been an inspirational lesson for me. Because of you I can live the life I live, that is the greatest gift any mother can give a child. To my sister,

Lori-Ann Ethier, you have been a shining example of what true faith is. You and I have traveled a million miles together.

To Timothy Morvan, your friendship, your strength, your love and your willingness to walk this journey with me has allowed me to fulfill my dreams. Thank you for being there.

And finally, my daughter Kaitlin, a gift touched by the hand of God whose words so profoundly spoken when she was six "Daddy, I believe in you," gave me wings. You are my heart, my soul, my light, my depth, my spirit and my love.

FOREWORD

How do you define heaven? Is it a real place or a state of mind? Is it only attainable as an after-death reward for a life well lived? Or can everyone be granted an entrance? Where is heaven? Does it reign eternal high up in the skies? Or can you access its glorious bounty while here on earth?

Questions like these have been debated throughout the ages, raising many more questions than there are answers. But one heavenly truth resonates clearly. Heaven is extraordinarily beautiful, a wonderful place so joyous, so full of unbridled happiness and divine love that even the mere thought of it can evoke a comforting feeling of inner peace and fulfillment unlike any other.

As a spiritual consultant and heavenly channel, Roland Comtois experiences the gift of heaven every day. It comes to him through spiritual messages that touch his heart and soul;

through angelic encounters with loving spirits; through signs sent from God, like the distinctive scent of cologne, a butterfly passing by at a strange moment, a flower in an unlikely place; and through channeled experiences that are truly life changing.

"Heaven is a place where peace and love exist...where you feel your truth and empowerment, a place where life continues for all who have departed before us."

"The beauty of heaven," says Roland, "is that it is there for everyone, at all times. It is a place where all the people on earth come together to finally celebrate life. It is a world of unseen love and energy, that, when touched, opens doors to unimaginable truths. As truly as it exists out there, it also resides within each of us and is all around us. We need simply to listen and believe. We need to live each moment in its entirety, to be grateful for today, and to love ourselves, and each other, unconditionally."

Endless possibilities for living a life beyond wonderful exist all around us. Roland started discovering these possibilities himself when he was just ten years old, with a visit from his grandmother shortly after her death. Three winged angels accompanied her to his bedroom that night, offering a young Roland a message of comfort and beauty that still nourishes his soul today. That was the first day in his journey as a channel, and from that day forward, his life would never be the same.

For years thereafter, Roland would feel the presence of other people or other things. Sometimes it came to him as a simple vibration or sensation that later escalated with sounds, sights and scents. As Roland listened more intently, these feelings evolved into direct communications with spirit: whispers at night, a brightly colored rainbow in a sun-filled sky, a sudden tear when God touched his heart, an instinctive knowing about the life of a complete stranger, messages from the departed eager to communicate with their loved ones on earth. The voices, the visions, the signs and the synchronicities that he calls coincidences, these are all an integral part of his life's mission as a spiritual medium, experiences that are as real as the ground he walks on.

Join Roland on his journey as an internationally renowned spiritual channel, as he shares experiences, messages and truths that are there to help and guide you on your life's path. Walk with him as he scales mountains with his faith; stand beside him as he goes forward into the unknown without fear; and hear what he hears from the breath of God.

He'll take you to his first visit with his departed grandmother, and to many spiritual encounters thereafter. He'll reveal the words of wisdom that encouraged him to believe and stay strong in the face of adversity, and continue to inspire him every day. And he'll show you what he saw and the love he felt as he climbed a brilliant white staircase to an angelic castle...*and then there was heaven.*

PROLOGUE

I HAVE SPENT A LIFETIME ministering to incredible people from all walks of life. I have been blessed to feel the love from those who have touched my life here in the physical realm and from those who have sent their love from the other side. I have helped souls cross over to heaven and have comforted loved ones remaining behind.

Inside, you will find a precious collection of inspirational messages and stories, many of which were channeled through divine energies from 1993 to 2008. The messages have been consistent and life changing for me. Words and phrases from days past to present moments and future experiences all serve as a source of inspiration in a time of great need.

Each experience has opened my heart to a new understanding of life and death, of heaven and earth, and the spiritual connections and synchronicities that bind us together. I did not write this book to convince you of my beliefs or to challenge your visions of a higher power. I merely offer them as a conduit for your healing and love.

God, by whatever name you may call him or her, speaks to all of us. Of that I am certain. Listen quietly from your sacred space and you will hear the sound of love.

You all have been blessed with amazing gifts, each of you with a particular way of expressing your gift. As you journey forward, revel in your own gladness of all the discoveries that await you. The discovery of the stillness is beautiful. Continue to nourish your soul. You are like still water that seems to sit quietly. The direction may be unclear now. Soon you'll know. The waters will flow again.

I received this message in 1995 when I was standing in silence at the edge of a New England pond. As I stood there, so many comforting truths came to mind and the peace was palpable. I remembered that in every instance of time, something beautiful occurs. I was reminded never to lose sight of life's simple pleasures and innate beauty, for they truly reflect the essence of a divine love.

The stillness of the pond was the perfect metaphor for the meaningful words I received that day and in the days that followed, and echoes the wisdom that has been implanted within each of us. If we are truly to be open to our own internal light and innate purpose, we must begin with faith.

Let your heart be held by love and feel the peace and the internal reservoir of sacredness that is within you. Have faith in yourself and your understanding of divinity, before you place your faith here or anywhere other than yourself.

Let your imagination take you to the pond of your memory and glide over it, absorbing as much love and energy as you can. Let the stillness encapsulate you. Let it enfold you and let it become you. Then, in that unseen stillness, your vision will be clear. And so much will be revealed to you.

Let your journey begin with this book.

It has been created to share with you the extraordinary messages that have touched and opened my heart to a greater understanding that we are truly not alone. These messages have been channeled from God, and from his band of angels, messengers and spirits, and they are all for you.

To help you navigate through this book, I

have italicized all of the messages that came to me in time of prayer and meditation. There are stories in this book as well, real life experiences that will help you foster a sense of belief that the light continues even after the demise of the physical body.

At the end of Chapter Seven, you will find sacred blank pages. These have been created for you through a vision that came to me long ago. I believe that if you place your hands upon these sacred blank pages, the words that have been recorded in this book will become a conscious part of your spirit, and you will be able to drink from its vibration.

I have been blessed to meet so many incredible people throughout my life who encouraged me to record my experiences here for all to share. I want to express my gratitude to them for allowing me to relate their personal stories on the following pages. Their grief over the loss of a loved one, their joy at making a connection and their love that truly transcends time and space is both poignant and inspirational, and stands as irrefutable testimony to the power of faith, hope and gratitude...and to the existence of heaven.

Thank you for giving me the privilege of sharing these messages and stories with you. It is my hope that what you read here will help to bring you closer to your divine source, to your angels and to your loved ones.

Blessings,

Roland M. Comtois

God is in here.

Spirit is in here.

Love is in here.

And they are all one and the same.

CONTENTS

ONE
A Journey of Love

TWO
A New Calling

THREE
Messages of Hope

FOUR
The Chalice

FIVE
Messages for Humanity

SIX
And Then There Was Heaven

SEVEN
The Book of Life

EIGHT
Making Their Way Home

NINE
Channeled Messages for the Soul

TEN
I Believe

ELEVEN
Beyond the Veil

TWELVE
A Grateful Heart

THIRTEEN
A Celebration of Angels

ONE

A JOURNEY OF LOVE

My journey as a channel began more than 36 years ago when my grandmother appeared in my room three days after she died, affirming a part of a story that is so much bigger than anyone can imagine. That story involves each one of us, joining us together with eternal bonds of love strung together through time, from here to heaven. Many people have asked me how I came to have this gift and my answer is always the same. We all have the ability to make spiritual connections and experience heaven if only we would listen to what's already inside of us.

Have you ever witnessed the joyful wisdom in the eyes of a newborn child? Babies enter the world with wide-eyed wonder, their eyes speaking volumes about a fantastic journey they just completed, as well as the one they are so eager to begin anew. They look around in pure amazement with an innate appreciation for all they see, thoughtfully drinking in every detail of their surroundings, every color, every shape, every scent and every possibility, like they were welcoming an old friend they dearly missed. If you look at the soulful gaze of a baby in their first few minutes of life, you can sense an unmistakable inner peace and knowing radiating from within, as if the very essence of someone vastly older, much wiser and more loving were peering back at you.

They say that children are born into this world directly from the heart of God to share a vision of love so abundant and nurturing that it is most definitely heaven sent. It is only through the effects of time

LOVE TRANSCENDS TIME AND SPACE

and distance, through life's challenges and their sometimes harsh realities, that this feeling of unconditional love, trust and divine faith fades and retreats into a part of the soul that can elude us during our journey on earth.

As adults, some of the most spiritual of us have been able to hold on to that memory of a place and existence so glorious that it seems truly unbelievable to others. I don't know why this is, but I am ever so grateful that I was able to keep this knowing alive even through the darkest moments of my life. I admit that my faith was tested time and time again by fear, by despair and by a sense of hopelessness that threatened to overwhelm my very being. But I survived them, not by sheer will alone, but by a spiritual understanding so ingrained within me that nothing can shake my belief that behind every cloud there is a rainbow, that in every instant of darkness there shines a light, and that in every feeling of uncertainty lies hope, one of the greatest gifts of all. I know, beyond any doubt, that each of us is blessed with the ability to connect to the vision of everlasting love that we were born with, any time, anywhere. We need only look inside and remember.

My mother used to tell me that I was one of the easiest babies to put to bed. She would no sooner lay me down in my crib than I would begin to smile and coo at the wall or the ceiling. She said she would shake her head in wonder at what amused me so, when the room was so obviously empty of anyone other than the two of us. Who —or what—comforted me in my room remained a mystery to her throughout my childhood, questions she quickly dismissed because they didn't have a plausible answer. She was much more comfortable thinking that I was perhaps a little different than other children, but that I was a good baby who didn't demand much from her at a time when she didn't have much to give. From the day she brought me home from the hospital through my toddler years and well beyond, she said I was never unhappy when left alone.

That's because I never was alone. None of us are. As far back as I can remember I felt an unconditional love from a heavenly presence much greater than anything else I have ever experienced. I would sense a flutter of energy, see a flash of light and just know that someone was there watching over me. I would catch sight of them out of the corner of my eye. Someone walking past me. Angels surrounding my bed at night. Spiritual beings and souls of all ages passing through the room. I could feel a loving hand on my heart and knew that someone was always standing nearby, always giving me support, courage and love. I felt it every day. And while my family never spoke of such things, I understood at a very young age that these heavenly visitors would always be there for me no matter what. I had no doubts about that. I also thought seeing angels and spirits was entirely normal too, for they were as real to me as the members of my family were.

It amazes me to observe the chi, or life essence of a young child. It's as if they see with the clarity that eludes their seniors. A child's magnificence illuminates a conscious connection between the spiritual realm and the physical world. It is more than apparent that most children have the insight of an old sage from long ago, gifted beyond a comprehension of this time, their hearts anchoring the divinity for many. When my daughter Kaitlin was born more than 16 years ago, she spent her first moments staring at me as if she had expected to see me there. Her eyes twinkled with such heavenly delight that I wept, and I wept until there were no tears left in me. I realized that in her gaze I saw the same loving eyes that used to tenderly watch over me as a baby.

I am reminded of a little girl I met once, not more than two years old, who would call out to her great-grandfather, a man she had never known in her lifetime. She would speak his name, point to him and laugh out loud as if they shared a private joke. It was as if he was right there in the room with her. By all accounts, he was there. Her vision was very real. So too was the presence of a young father whose life was taken in a tragic car accident months before his daughter was born. Not long after she was born, his baby girl would smile, laugh and stare at the easy chair in her nursery, acknowledging the unseen energy of her father, now a guardian angel watching over her from the other side. Their mothers had asked me if their departed loved ones knew about their children. I told them it was much greater than that, their babies also knew about them.

I was still a child when I first realized not everyone saw or felt the same things I did. I was playing with my cousins, when one of them suggested that we hold a séance to contact the other side. A séance, by definition, promises untold powers with a supernatural ability to answer questions and receive answers and messages from the other side. But why would you need to hold a séance to communicate with spirits, I wondered? I already knew that I could talk to spirits whenever I wanted; to me it was never a question. Couldn't everyone hear them as I did? What was the big deal anyway?

As my older cousins and I were all gathered around the table trying to contact the other side, I started pointing out the spirits who were standing around the room. Don't you see them too, I asked with all the innocence of a small child? They responded with laughter, and I remember thinking that they took great delight in teasing and taunting me about my imaginary friends. To them, this was just a game until they realized that I was completely serious. Maybe it was the look in my eyes or the sincere way I spoke about what I saw that made them uncomfortable even though they insisted they didn't believe me. I guess when it hit them that there might actually be "ghosts" standing among us they became unnerved, wanting nothing more to do with the séance or me. Things never seemed the same after that.

It is at such times that many children who see spirits—or imaginary playmates as their parents or teachers are more comfortable calling them—stop acknowledging their presence to avoid being ridiculed. I was no different. I kept my visions to myself for a long time after that, trying to fit in with my friends and family and not risking their name-calling. I have to tell you that keeping these spiritual experiences to myself was not easy, for they were—and still are—truly extraordinary. No matter how often I witness them, they send chills of affirmation up and down my spine. They are always amazing.

The truth about spiritual communication is that once we simplify our lives and recognize that relationships with our departed loved ones still exist (certainly in a very different way than what we are used to), then we can manifest the ability to see beyond the veil of time and space. You just have to believe. The ability to communicate with them is not defined by religious traditions or some other form of structure, but by something completely innate...faith. In the stillness of your mind, heart and soul the sacred relationships that were formed during your lifetime continue. With commitment, consistency, and devotion you can begin the process of crafting and expanding a beautiful more loving experience with those loved ones you have lost. Children do that instinctively, and so can you.

RELATIONSHIPS WITH OUR DEPARTED LOVED ONES STILL EXIST

No matter what curve balls life throws at you, there is always a miracle right around the corner. My father walked out on my family when

I was only 10 years old, but I felt much older, with the weight of the world on my shoulders. I remember following him down to the end of the driveway that last day, struggling to carry his suitcase for him. I wanted to believe he was just going off on a short adventure, but the truth of it was my parents were getting a divorce. It was only after he missed my birthday and Christmas a few years in a row that I would accept the fact that he had left for good. Looking back on it now, I have only the vaguest memories of life with him. I know that he was a musician and he liked to sing and we went out for pizza now and then, but that's all I can recall.

THERE IS A MIRACLE AROUND EVERY CORNER

My grandmother Isabelle died soon thereafter and life changed dramatically for me and my family. I found comfort again when I least expected it, in the solitude of my room where love had never failed to surround me when I was just a baby.

I remember it as if it had happened yesterday. It was 11:59 PM. I was in our second floor apartment, in the middle bedroom in my bed, which was in the middle of the room. To the right of my bed was a window with blue curtains.

I had retreated to my room in hopes of finding my childhood wishes tucked within my dreams, but this night would be like no other. There through the window came a stream of white light so brilliant and dazzling that I think I rubbed my eyes several times to see if I was dreaming. I wasn't. The light, I remember so clearly, was filled with warmth as it cascaded down from the heavens like a luminous silk scarf flowing in the wind, passing through my window to the end of my bed. In an instant, my grandmother, Isabelle, was standing there. She was glowing in this sparkling light from the tips of her toes to the top of her head and I could feel her energy and her love as if she and her angels were actually wrapping their arms around me in a heartfelt embrace. What impressed me so was that her hair was still as white and pure as snow, as it was in life. It was astonishing to actually see her standing there looking just like she always did. Then she spoke, giving me a message that would ultimately make all the difference in my life.

"Roland, you will see things, hear things and feel things. Don't be afraid. You will be all right."

Three of the most magnificent angels you could ever have imagined with gossamer wings stood behind her, their airy feet suspended off the ground. I was in complete awe of their beauty and grace and how they made me feel inside: calm, safe and very much protected. They were dressed in golden hues and radiant beams of light, which embraced everything in the room, including me. I felt no fear. I was enveloped in peace and love. I remember feeling that the angels and my grandmother shared a kinship that transcended time and place and I was so glad to know that she was not alone. It was so beautiful to witness and so comforting to know that I was a part of this.

HEAVEN IS IN ALL THINGS, IN ALL PLACES, AND ALL EVENTS

When my grandmother stood there adorned in the light of heaven, I somehow understood that heaven is in all things, in all places and all events. I learned from that moment that I could find my heaven here amidst the suffering of my father's departure, my mother's grief and the worry and responsibility I now felt for my little sister, Lori. I'm not telling you that I didn't cry over my situation. I did for years, and years, and each time I came to a desperate moment, something picked me up and moved me through the turmoil to a place of ease. Actually, as I am remembering this part of my story for this book, I'm crying right now. Even now the voice of hope resonates through me, giving me the same courageous cloak of love as it did so many years ago. We all come to certain places in our lives that require delving deep within the root of knowing, and from there we can survive. I believe that in this place our spiritual associations with God, angels, spirits, departed loves and ourselves, exist.

Amazingly, that moment took place over thirty-six years ago. That was the beginning of a remarkable spiritual connection to the divine entities, to God, to my guardian angels and to all those parted loved ones that cared for me and for so many others. That was also the first time that I truly began to believe that there really was a place called heaven.

No longer could I deny feeling the presence of other people or other things not of this world. Sometimes it started with a vibration, then the sensation would escalate with sounds, sights and aromas. The journey of a channel, as I know now, is about being a beacon of love. I know that somewhere, somehow, I signed a spiritual contract to make this my calling. But during those tender years of my youth, I decided to keep this a secret tucked safely away within, daring not to risk revealing it to those who did not believe.

Soon after my father left us, I took on

the role of parent for my younger sister and my distraught mother. Money was tight and we had to leave our comfortable middle-class apartment and move to low-income housing in the tenements of Woonsocket, Rhode Island. Hard as our life had become, bitterness and despair could not find a home in my heart. I always knew my angels and so many others were with me. They gave me strength in the face of adversity. They gave me the courage to go to school each day, avoiding the dreaded bullies who would grab my glasses right off my face and hurl them to the ground where they shattered into jagged pieces. They gave me the motivation at age 14 to get a summer job as a camp counselor so that I could help my mother put food on the table. I made $60 a week in those days, and gave my mother $45 of it.

Times were tough, especially for my mother. While I was blessed with an entourage of angelic support, my mother battled the demons of depression and fell apart under the strain. It was after a troubled romance that left her with yet another broken heart that she took to her bed and tried to will herself away. I did my best to cheer her and tend to her needs, but soon realized that she needed more help than I alone could give her. She had become weak with sorrow and despair that turned on her beautiful body like an illness until she became almost lifeless. One day she looked particularly ashen as I left for school. She whispered that she might not be here when I came home, she felt so bad. Her words were like a corkscrew in my soul. I knew I had to do something to ease her pain so I turned to prayer like I never had before. I asked God, the universe, and my grandmother for their divine help, and called on every angelic being I could think of to send my mother and me a miracle.

I came home from school that day to find my mother more at peace. It wasn't long before she left her bed and returned to her daily routine. I was delighted that life once again coursed through her body and that she came back to my sister and me. Seeing her recover shortly after I prayed for her life confirmed what I had always known deep inside—that our loved ones, the angels, and the universal supreme light are always there to share their love and support with us. I had asked for spiritual assistance for my mother, and my prayers were answered.

I, too, continued in my daily routine after that spending my days going from school to my part-time job to home in that troubled Woonsocket neighborhood. But, unlike the many other underprivileged children who learned to tough it out on the streets each day with little hope for the future, eating disappointment for breakfast, lunch and dinner, I knew in my heart that something magical was right around the corner.

As I walked to school each day, past gangs of thugs and the rundown apartment buildings littered with garbage and broken dreams, I would walk by a magnificent church where I could often hear music and singing...and then there was heaven.

Up until now, this church, St. Charles, had not been a part of my life. That, too, was about to change. I started to go to church by myself every Sunday, walking alone to this wonderful refuge. While I enjoyed everything about these Sunday morning services, it was the music that took hold of my soul and I knew what drew me here. I wanted to sing! I wasn't content just singing with the congregation, I wanted to join the beautiful chorus of voices that filled every ounce of my being with pure joy. So I made it a point to befriend the choir director and soon I was a member of the church choir, proudly raising my voice to the heavens for every Sunday and holiday service.

Singing gave my life a whole new purpose. I began to think how much it meant to me and wondered if it could make a difference in the lives of the children who lived around me in the tenements. Like me, they were living in a broken household with a single parent, where love and happiness were often scarce companions. Some had it much worse than me and were growing up alone, often full of fear, tiptoeing around an alcoholic father or an abusive mother so as not to elicit their undeserved wrath. I thought they might enjoy the happiness that's inherent in singing, so I decided to form my own children's choir. My idea was to invite these children who had nothing to give a gift of love to others in need, specifically the elderly residents of local nursing homes.

It wasn't easy trying to recruit singers from my tough inner city neighborhood. Here I was, a bespectacled teenage boy, not at all athletic in a sports-minded community, who wanted to gather together young people to sing in a choir in their spare time. This was surely a test of faith perhaps even greater than speaking of visions during that fateful séance session as a child and one that took an inordinate amount of perseverance.

One by one, I approached the children. Many walked away, scoffing at my plans. Some mocked me, especially the boys already hardened by life on the streets. But some, shyly at first, were intrigued and before I knew it, I had become the choir director for 14 girls and one boy, ages 4 to 19. We all faced teasing by the other kids who lived in our rough area, but we didn't care. We just cared about singing. Together, we marched into the musty cellar of one of the tenements, brushed away the cobwebs, put up some paneling, cleaned up a corner and began singing. We practiced day and night, whenever we could. I eagerly took on the role of singing teacher, and armed with techniques I had learned at church, I taught the children to sing. I was so moved by the purity and sweetness of their voices, I christened our group the "Singing Hearts Choir." And, in November, just a few months after we formed our group, we performed at our first nursing home.

Our choir drew quite a following as we sang our hearts out for some of the most appreciative audiences I would ever have the honor of meeting. Little did they realize that the happy smiles on their faces as we sang to them were teaching each of us some of the most important of life's lessons, for while we were

TO GROW IN A SPIRITUAL WAY YOU MUST GIVE OF YOURSELF

singing, we were giving them the greatest gift of all, the gift of love. And that gift was returned to us one-hundred-fold along with something else we had yet to experience in our lives, the healing power of gratitude.

To grow in a spiritual way, you must give of yourself. Through the "Singing Hearts Choir," we rose above the impoverished conditions of our homes and the frailty of our lives to be granted abundance in so many ways, none of which was material. The grateful eyes that watched us as we were singing were filled with unbridled love and for some in the choir it was not a recognizable look. Our elderly fans held our hands and our hearts as we sang, sometimes off key, and still loved us exactly as we were. Many tried to share their gratitude with words, but age and illness had silenced their voices, so they touched us with genuine compassion and nothing divided us. The power of sharing yourself with someone else can truly be transformational, like the calm that always comes after a dark and turbulent storm. It's in you.

The local press began to take notice of us, too. Articles and photos announced our debut at elderly centers and nursing homes around town. One reporter summed up my goals in a short list when he first heard about my plans for a choir.

He wrote, "Roland's list is only four items.

But what a tall order. First, Roland would like to establish a loving relationship between the elderly of Greater Woonsocket and some of the area's younger generation. Then, he would like to find some means of eliminating the sadness and loneliness old people often face. Next, Roland would like to provide an opportunity for children from families from less affluent neighborhoods a chance to grow and learn about love and sharing. And, finally he would like to brighten the holiday season for the elderly by giving love and smiles."

He went on to say that when he first heard of my idea, he wished me luck and "within myself I figured his plan to be a long shot. Now I'm a believer. They say some of the greatest stories come out of the most unlikely of places and under the thinnest of circumstances. And that's the situation with this story, a story about the 'Singing Hearts Choir.' "

In his article, he spoke of my next wish, to acquire community support in order to purchase red robes. Donations flowed in and we were able to raise the money to purchase fabric. My aunt made the robes by hand, sewing white hearts on each of them to symbolize our combined efforts to extend our hearts for the purest of reasons.

During the next three years, our choir made lots of people smile, bringing love to those who were living out the end of their lives while giving hope to the ones who were just starting out. I was especially affected by our ability to make a difference in people's lives and knew without hesitation that I wanted to dedicate my life to helping others.

I had taken a job in an auto parts store after school, working my way up to assistant manager. The men I worked with were not the singing type; many were angry and prone to cussing out their customers, as well as each other, instead of making them happy. One day I had had enough. I had begun to despise this job and decided that I couldn't spend my time like this any longer. I quit on the spot and headed over to one of the nursing homes where the "Singing Hearts" had performed, where I boldly asked for a job and got one.

Working at the nursing home put me into contact with so many great people who were all driven by the power of friendship and compassion. My patients were grateful for my company and any kindness I could bestow on them. Many of their families, if they had any, appreciated sharing the burden of their care with me and the other staff members. I became close to many of the patients and their loved ones, making connections that would eventually change my life.

From the time my grandmother had visited me with her angels and through my high school years, I continued to have visions and contacts with the other side. As difficult as it was, I kept these experiences quiet, not giving in to them, not sharing them with anyone except my cousin Debby and my friend Beverly. Debby was the only one of my family who believed me so long ago during that childhood séance and she faithfully kept my confidences in her heart. Beverly, always supportive, would record my visions in a notebook, keeping them safe until the time that I was ready to grow into this amazing power. That day came quite suddenly while I was driving a friend to the hospital.

I had become friends with a woman I met when I was a camp counselor for her children. She and her boyfriend, Henry, a high school English teacher, and I would spend hours on end talking about life, the choices we made, and the decisions that made us truly happy. Henry became somewhat of a father figure to me, eagerly dispensing advice about my future. Knowing how much I enjoyed helping others, he encouraged me to go to college to earn a degree in nursing, something that had never even entered my mind. Growing up on welfare, without a father, and with a mother too worn down by life to discuss such matters, college was not an option for me. Or so I believed until Henry guided me through the application process, cheering me on whenever I became discouraged.

The news that Henry had cancer came out of the blue and hit me like a thunderbolt. Our visits grew shorter as he grew frailer by the day, weakened by the continuous chemically induced assaults of his chemotherapy treatments. I am grateful that no matter how busy I was or how ill he felt, we always made time to connect. As it turns out, I was there when he needed me most, for I was the one who drove him to the hospital for the very last time.

"Roland, I think it's my time to go," he said as I entered his room. His breathing was labored, his skin, ashen. The cancer had ravaged his 6 foot 4 inch frame, leaving him too weak to walk or even stand up. I helped him up from his bed, supporting him on my back, as I assured him that I would take him to the hospital. His arms dangled loosely over my much smaller frame, now buckling under the weight of his immobile body. His once sure-footed legs dragged listlessly behind mine as I struggled to carry him, step by step, to my waiting car.

I didn't try to deny his solemn words. We both knew it was his time.

A single tear rolled down his sunken cheek

as he told me that he had never been any good at telling people how much he loved them. In that moment, he was thinking about his children whom he had emotionally abandoned years before.

"I'm afraid to go," he cried, his voice now nothing more than an anguished whisper. And then he couldn't find the strength to talk anymore.

"You don't have to be afraid," I said to him as he leaned against my shoulder for support as I drove him to the hospital. "I know you are going to be all right."

I told him that I knew about heaven and that he was going to be embraced with love and healing when he got there. I told him that love never dies and will always connect us to the ones we love, both in heaven and here on earth. I told him not to fear, but to go forward into that beautiful light without regrets.

SYNCHRONICITIES ARE PART OF THE HEAVENLY PLAN

Henry died a few days later. It was a peaceful death that turned out to be a beautiful moment for him. I don't believe in coincidences.

I believe that everything happens for a reason and that these synchronicities, as I like to call them, are an important part of the heavenly plan.

My friendship—and my last visit with Henry—was not by chance, as I learned definitively some twenty years after his death.

I was doing a private reading for a young woman in my office in Rhode Island. I had never met her before and didn't know anything about her or her life. Her reading began normally, with messages that appeared to me as they do during such sessions. Yet as I was counseling her, Henry suddenly appeared and stood by her shoulder. I started shouting with the excitement reserved for seeing old friends.

"Henry is here! I can't believe it! Henry is here!"

The young woman looked startled, then listened intently when I relayed Henry's message to her.

"Please tell my daughter I am sorry that I wasn't there for her when she was growing up. Please tell her how much I love her and that I have always loved her even though I wasn't very good at telling her. Please tell her that I am sorry for abandoning her."

And then he turned to me and said, "Thank you for holding me up that day."

He told me about all the love he received when he left and that my words of comfort had meant so much to him.

The young woman in my office began to cry and I cried right along with her as I told her what her father was saying. "Your father loved you, Susan. That's why you came here today. So you could hear that your father loved you!"

Susan told me that she had never really gotten to know her father; there always seemed such an impenetrable barrier between them. He was cold, distracted and not home much. When he was home, he never seemed to have time for her. She missed having the kind of dad she longed for as she was growing up, the kind of loving father her friends had. She carried her sadness with her to my office that day.

As unbelievable as it was, I told her that I had become friends with her father towards the end of his life and that I was the one who drove him to the hospital that last time. She said she had wished it had been her driving the car that day; she would have liked to be given the chance to say goodbye. After hearing his message to her, she left my office with a joyful heart and with a gift of love she would always cherish from a father she truly missed.

What began with two strangers meeting for the first time in my office ended with the realization that Henry had impacted both our lives at different times. As he neared the end of his life, Henry carried with him the deep regret of emotionally abandoning his family, and his daughter Susan. It all came together for him at the end, when he realized how much he loved his children. I was glad that I was able to pass those sentiments along.

My role in this was to act as a spiritual conduit between father and daughter, sharing messages of love between heaven and earth. This session also had an important message of healing for me, as many of my future readings would as well. I told Susan that I too had been abandoned by my father and I knew her pain. We both began to heal that day.

Shortly after Henry died, I took his advice and enrolled in college to study nursing. My life's journey was about to take another turn toward heaven.

TWO

A NEW CALLING

I STARTED NURSING CLASSES at the Community College of Rhode Island in September of 1984 and they were everything I dreamed they would be. Challenging, rewarding, exhausting. While the technical training was at first mind-boggling, the patient care was food for my soul. I found my place among my fellow students, all of us eager to put into practice the new skills we learned each day. As the bonds of friendship grew within my class, I became more comfortable about sharing the messages I received from the spiritual realm. For the first time in my life, I left the doubts that had plagued my childhood behind, and began to use my gifts as they were intended to be used.

Before long, I started channeling for my classmates. At first, I just called upon the universe to help us get good grades after all the time we spent studying. I would gather my classmates together for a prayer session before an exam. Those who didn't believe in this kind of thing wouldn't join us. Those who did would stand with me in a circle and we'd make our connection. Those prayers worked and helped us succeed in this very intensive nursing program. But it wasn't our prayers alone that did the trick. It was a combination of hard work, of our belief in ourselves and our unyielding faith in the power of spiritual collaboration that helped us achieve what we needed. No matter what your goal, it will work its magic in your life and help you realize everything you could ever hope for.

Later, I started to do readings during lunch breaks and in between exams for the kids in my class whom I became closest to. I would share messages with them, helping them navigate through the challenges of their lives.

Back in those early days of my career as a medium, I did readings with a regular deck of cards, more for the comfort of the people I was meeting with rather than as tools for myself. If you have never had a reading before, it can be a little disconcerting to have someone start talking about personal things in your life and loved ones who may have passed. Working with cards somehow makes the process easier to understand and accept, as if the cards themselves were telling a story. Actually, they do. In the beginning when I was first learning how to share my gifts, I would receive visions of what each card meant during a dream, signs that I took to be a subconscious nudging from above for me to use my intuitive talents. So as I set out to do my first personal readings, I would bring along a deck of cards, have my "clients" shuffle them, and lay them out in the pattern revealed to me during my visions.

All I had to do was look at the cards that I had spread out on the table and they would tell me a story about the person sitting in front of me. I was always as amazed as they were with the personal messages I relayed, for I could feel a special healing taking place within their souls during these sessions. I did card readings for years while my abilities continued to evolve. I went from working with cards to painting the auras I would see around my clients. Auras, as you may know, reflect the energy fields that emanate from each one of us. These energy fields vibrate with different colors that vary with the individual's physical, emotional, mental and spiritual states. With practice, everyone can see auras. I was able to do so early on, using this ability as a window to their soul to help pass on healing energy. My abilities progressed to simply knowing in my heart and soul what the person sitting in front of me needed to hear. Now when I hold a person's hand, I actually see a virtual movie playing before my eyes, and I relate their story as I hear and experience it.

Between studying and doing spiritual readings for friends and clients, my time in school was over almost as quickly as it started. Before I knew it, I was giving the commencement speech at our graduation. While I was thrilled with all that I had accomplished during my nursing studies, I felt torn between embarking on a professional career as a nurse or working as a spiritual consultant to help heal people's souls.

I needn't have worried, for as quickly as the doubts made themselves at home in my thoughts, I was in for another of life's lessons. In order to become a licensed nurse, all nursing school graduates had to pass a state board exam. I certainly didn't think this would be a problem because I had aced all my courses in school. But the universe had other plans for me and I was in for a large dose of humility.

I had studied hard and was well prepared for the exam, or so I thought. When the scores were issued, I found that I was a mere four points short of receiving certification. I had already accepted a full-time job as a nurse, and everyone around me, including my employer and my coworkers, didn't give my passing the required exam another thought. But I didn't pass it. I couldn't believe it. How was I going to explain my failure to them, to my friends and family? I was mortified at the very thought of it.

I'm not sure who said, "when you are down to nothing, God is up to something" but those words always seem to ring true and certainly did so that night. In need of some comforting, I decided to lose my sorrows in a big spaghetti dinner. I set out a pot of water to boil and I turned my attention to a can of tomato sauce. No sooner had I opened one end of the can when the sauce shot out with a life of its own and splattered all over the ceiling. **BE** "What next!" I asked to no one **STILL** in particular as I climbed on top **AND** of the table and reached up with a paper towel to clean the sauce **LISTEN** off the ceiling. Then it happened. I fell and landed hard right on my knee, rendering it and me virtually immobile for the next seven days.

I was forced to be still and listen for an entire week. I listened with an intensity that I never knew was possible. And I prayed, a lot. In so doing, I learned one of most fundamental truths of my journey...that the only way to grow spiritually is to be silent...and I received one of the most important gifts of all, the gift of humility.

I lost my footing, if you will, in October, and did not go back to work again until the following spring after retaking the state nursing certification exam. I was still belaboring my decision of whether to be a full-time nurse or a spiritual conduit, but I needed to earn a living for my family and myself. Like many who are considering taking a risk and following their passion or choosing the safer route and earn a steady paycheck, I chose the paycheck.

I thrived in my new role as a nurse, eagerly ministering to the ill and infirm. But in spite of the personal and professional satisfaction I derived from my job, I still wondered if I was fulfilling my true destiny. I was working more than forty hours a week, and no matter how physically and emotionally draining my days were, I continued to do readings for people in my free time after work. Some took place at house parties where I would do readings for four or five people. Other times I would drive to someone's home for a personal session. These experiences always resonated within me, especially when grieving families called me to their homes. I started to look forward to them as much as I did taking care of my patients.

It was during the first of these after-work

readings that I had my first powerful experience dealing with someone else's overwhelming grief over the death of a loved one. I was driving from Providence to my new clients' house in Fall River and I had to cross over a bridge. As I was driving over the bridge, I felt a strong spiritual energy and had vivid visions of a bright red altar, surrounded by lots of religious articles and burning candles, including a statue of Mary. There were photos on it too, framed pictures of Jesus and a handsome young man. I instantly knew there was a lot of sorrow surrounding that altar, and I felt it just as strongly as if whatever happened there had happened to me.

When I arrived at the house, my clients led me into the living room, and right there in a corner of that room was the red altar exactly as it had appeared to me in my vision. My clients had built that altar there in honor of their son who had died unexpectedly some months earlier. I knew at once that the energy I had experienced in the car as I drove over the bridge was their son. He had appeared to me during my car ride and I recognized him immediately when I saw a photograph of him on the red altar. I was able to put his parents' hearts at ease when I relayed his messages to them, that he was fine and at peace on the other side. Their son's messages helped to diminish their grief, and to reassure them that love does not die with the person. After that, they called me routinely to check in with their boy, to make sure that everything was settled with him and that he was doing all right in heaven.

It was around the same time when I was summoned to another woman's house. We sat together at her kitchen table and I started to tell her this amazing story about her life. As I spoke, I saw the spirits of three little girls surrounding her. I learned that all three of her girls had died a year apart from each other in freakish events. She sat there and listened to the stories that I told her about how unexpectedly each loss had come, and she sighed deeply as if she was trying to just catch her breath. I described each of her three girls as I saw them, one with her curly hair, one who had glasses on, and the other with braces on her teeth. There weren't any photographs in the room for me to have known what the girls looked like, so as I described them in detail, their mother knew in her heart that her girls were right there with her. While this experience could not take away her pain, for it was so great a loss, it did begin to heal her broken heart. What was really most astounding to me was that this woman had more courage than any other person I had ever met in my life. After our session, I learned that she had survived the incomprehensible loss of her only three children to go on to help other people with their grief.

Dealing with death was a routine part of my job. As a licensed nurse, I was trained to know the signs of impending death, physical symptoms that very clearly predict that the end of life is near. But I also had the innate knowing on both an emotional and spiritual level when my patients were getting ready to go. I would make it a point to support those patients who were about to pass over, comforting and praying with them as they made this transition.

One day when I was making my rounds, I felt a tingling as I entered the room of an elderly woman under my care. Grace was an Alzheimer's patient who was in her late 90s. She had never uttered a coherent word during all the time I had ministered to her, or looked with any sign of recognition into my eyes. I never had the chance to learn what she was like before that devastating illness took over her mind and her life because she had outlived all her relatives. For the most part, she had no visitors except the nursing home staff who tended to her out of duty rather than friendship.

So that day when I felt that tell-tale tingling, I sensed that it was her time and that it was important that I call the staff together so we could stay with her as she made her way to the other side. The staff and I had become her family; our familiar voices would support her as she made her transition to the other side. I gently placed my stethoscope upon her chest and quietly counted as I listened to her heart slow down from 160 to 80 to 30 to 5, 4, 3, 2, 1, and then she was gone. At that moment, I saw her leave her physical body and, most amazingly, watched as she was lifted right out that captive disease-ridden prison that had held her for so many empty years. She looked back at me and smiled as she went to the other side.

Scenes like this were often repeated when I witnessed a patient's last breaths on earth, and even one memorable time when I wasn't physically present. I was making my rounds, checking on patients when I entered Emile's room to make sure he was comfortable. It was readily apparent when I came closer to his body that he had already passed. Shaken and inconsolable at the thought of him passing on alone, I left his room and sat outside on a bench, praying and asking for the angels to bless him on his journey. No sooner had I asked, then my prayers were answered and

Emile stood before me and spoke.

"I am not what you see in the bed. I am free. I am free."

Then I watched as he joyfully walked into the light.

My patients became like family to me, and I to them. As often as possible, I would stand vigil with them when the end was near. I would gather the nursing staff together so we could nurture their physical body with a comforting touch and a kind word. We'd give them spiritual support with our prayers of hope and light, gently supporting them as they crossed into the light. Frequently I would see them actually leave their physical body.

I remember when a woman named Mary was near death and I was there to comfort both her and her daughter during this intensely moving time. Her daughter had taken wonderful care of her mother while she was a patient of ours, spending most of her time at her bedside. Mary had been very sick with a debilitating illness and had great difficulty speaking, so her daughter and I would always be the ones talking in her room. After Mary passed, I lost touch with her daughter who had been a regular visitor at the nursing home, until several years later when she came to me for a reading.

She looked familiar to me when she came

for her session but I couldn't quite place her. Her husband had died a few months earlier and she had come to me hoping for a message from him. As I began the reading, in came her mother Mary talking like she never wanted to stop talking. In life, I remembered, she couldn't get the words out, and now she was making up for lost time.

After she thanked her daughter for taking such good care of her during her illness, she told me how grateful she was for the kindness of our nursing staff during her last months on earth. I felt blessed by her appreciation.

Mary's appearance was soon followed by a gentleman whose message made little sense to me, but it meant everything to Mary's daughter.

He exclaimed, "Oh my God, I love how the staircase is decorated." Listening to his words, I described the garlands and other Christmas decorations that so delighted him, relating accurate details of the festive holiday décor that graced the home they had shared for so many years. Unbeknownst to me, Christmas had been one of their favorite times of the year, when together they turned their home into a showcase of yuletide spirit. Mary's daughter gasped upon hearing the message, knowing in her heart that her beloved husband was truly making a connection in that moment. She had come to me hoping to receive a message, and what she heard was music to her soul.

The messages that come to me are often fragmented much like what you would read in a telegram. Telegrams, by their very nature, are brief, often communicating a direct message that only the reader would understand. A telegram may direct the recipient to "meet me at noon tomorrow," omitting where the meeting was to take place. It is up to the recipient to put the pieces together. So it is with the messages I share, they often only make sense to the person for whom they were intended.

Mary's non-stop talking and message of thanks meant so much to me and her daughter, but her husband's words, which I did not understand, were just what she alone needed to hear.

Of all my patients that I loved and cared for at the nursing home, Florence was a particular favorite. At age 94, her zest for life never diminished, even though she could no longer see or walk. She was confined to a wheelchair but she never complained. Her face would light up at the sound of my voice, arms extended to embrace me with a heartfelt hug. We used to talk together about my life and hers, sharing our stories and dreams about the future. She was especially excited about my upcoming wedding, her face glowing with happiness just at the thought of it. She used to tell me that she was not going to miss it for the world and that she would dance with me on my big day. Even as she became more frail and edged ever closer to death, she would whisper her promise to me. The day of her death came too soon, weeks before my wedding. I had made it a priority to be with her when she took her final breath, so that I could support her and pray with her as she passed over. At that last moment, I watched as Florence regained the strength in spirit that she had lost during life and actually stood up and walked to the other side. Not surprisingly, I did feel her presence at my wedding, standing proud just like she said she would during the ceremony and dancing with pure joy at the reception.

It isn't only just older people who send me messages from other side. It is babies too. On that trip to Fall River where I met with the parents who prayed for their departed son at their red altar, I also felt the energy of a tiny baby who had died at a tender young age. When that baby appeared to me as I was driving in my car, even without words I knew he was asking me to deliver a message for him. After my first session that evening in Fall River, I was scheduled to attend a house party where I met with a young couple who were clearly grieving. As soon as they sat down for our session, I told them that I had seen their baby boy. He was surrounded by love in heaven; bands of angels were looking after him now. Their healing began with that message, for they needed to know, above all else, that their little one was not alone and was being loved and cared for in heaven.

All of these incidents clearly proved to me and to so many of my clients that heaven most certainly exists for everyone, from the very young to the very old. I know now, after more than 30 years of doing this work, that one special angel is sent to accompany each little child on his or her soul journey to heaven. I know that even the smallest baby is never alone during this transition. They are embraced by love in the moments before they pass and in all the moments thereafter. There is no question about this.

Since those early experiences, I have found that the messages I share with people allow them to finally catch their breath because of the things that they were able to hear. The grieving parents wanted reassurance that their son had made it to the other side. The young couple at the house party needed to know that their baby was in heaven before they could move on from their grief. The messages I receive are intended to help the recipient transition to the next step on their life's journey.

When I did my readings with the nursing staff on my lunch breaks at work, I would tell them their stories. Many would cry as they felt the energy in the room during these sessions. They would come back to me later and thank me, saying that what I had told them really made sense and the spirits that I saw, their loved ones who had passed, would have been the ones who would have come back to help them. Their gratitude overwhelmed me.

MESSAGES ARE A REFLECTION OF WHAT THE SOUL NEEDS

The messages I receive during personal readings continue to inspire a sense of healing and peace both within me and the people I read for. Without exception, I have found that the messages have a real purpose and come about because a part of their soul needs to hear it. Otherwise, the messages would not have come. The messages are usually a reflection of what they need and what I need to hear too. I have had the blessing of healing myself through my clients, opportunities for which I am eternally grateful. And equally important, I know that my clients are always there for a reason. Our sessions do not occur solely by happenstance. Rather, it is divine intervention that we have come together.

I had been working as a practical nurse for years when I decided to go back to school to earn an advanced designation as an RN, or registered nurse. If I was to channel all my energies to a career of healing, I intended to learn all that I could. I had just been nominated as "Long Term Care Nurse of the Year" in recognition of my compassion and commitment to the nursing profession, so going back to school made perfect sense to me. What I hadn't yet fully realized was that my gift of healing was destined to be of a spiritual nature, not a physical one.

Working towards that advanced nursing degree did not have the same impact on my life as I had expected. Instead, I found myself becoming more interested in doing readings than working as a nurse. I still enjoyed the patient care, but I somehow did not feel that I was following my path. Something was missing and I needed to reassess my goals. So I turned to God, the angels and the universe and asked what my role in life was supposed to be. And then quite clearly, I heard the answer.

Yours is not to heal the physical. Your mission is to heal the spirit.

So I left nursing school, only one semester course short of earning my RN. Needing to earn a living, I applied for and began working as a legislative outreach coordinator for a nursing organization setting up nursing programs in long-term care settings, only to spend more and more of my free time doing readings with the woman who hired me. She also had the gift, and although I did not know it at the time, I was guided there to stand in my truth so I could really see who I was.

STAND

IN

YOUR

TRUTH

We would start the day reading angel cards and sharing our intuitive abilities with each other and with a growing number of clients.

In those days, I would charge just a nominal fee for a reading, if anything at all. Surely, I could not support myself this way I thought. As my job grew tedious, I focused more and more of my energies on the spiritual realm. After spending two years working with this organization, I again wondered what I was supposed to be doing with my life. And once again, I asked God and my angels for their guidance.

I've been taught so many lessons in my journey as a channel, not the least of which is that we all need to ask for help from time to time. There is one important caveat to asking for guidance, however, and that is, when you ask the question, you must be prepared to listen to the answer.

I remember sitting at my desk and praying to my spiritual team to tell me who I was and what I should be doing in my life. I implored them to tell me what I needed to do next. The words came to me very clearly.

It is time to quit your job.

And so I contemplated that for a moment or two. "I can't quit my job," I said. I had responsibilities. I was a father. I had a family and a daughter who depended on me. I had rent and bills to pay. If I quit my job, how was I to survive financially?

And then I heard, with incredible stillness and power—

It is time to quit your job.

So I did. I went from my desk to my boss's desk and gave her my two weeks' notice. She looked surprised and asked me what I was planning to do. I had but a vague idea. I knew that I was being led. And there was something else I was supposed to do.

As I packed up my belongings and got into my car, I admittedly felt doubts and not a little bit of fear. What had I done? What was I going to do? Was I crazy to be so impulsive? But instead of letting my fear control me, I listened to my inner voice, and let myself be guided by the voice of faith, belief, and trust.

For many of us it can be hard to distinguish between wishful thinking and a message. When spirit speaks, you feel a calming sensation. Fear, anxiousness, and restlessness are not part of the divine energy. Unfortunately, many of us in times of turmoil and uncertainty give power to these stressful emotions, and unwittingly negate messages from our inner voice, from spirit. It can be difficult to follow your heart's desire, but that is ultimately where your journey should take you.

I got in my car and started driving toward my daughter's school to pick her up. I wasn't sure why, but before I knew it, I pulled up in front of a building that had a "for rent" sign in front of it. It was in a town called Harmony, and it was located on a Christmas tree farm.

I parked the car and went up to a man I saw walking on the property. We struck up a conversation and I asked him how much the rent was.

He answered saying, "rent is $400 a month. No deposit, no security. Rent is due on the first of every month. If that's agreeable to you, you can move in tomorrow."

All I had was $400 in cash. I had no money for the second or third month's rent but I knew that God had big plans for me. I gave that man all the money I had right on the spot and I opened up the "Hands Of Light Reiki Center" the next day. It was an eye-opening experience as I realized that I was on my way to achieving something bigger than I had ever imagined.

One of the most amazing aspects of life is that we have the opportunity to manifest the things we need. It requires a steadfast commitment to knowing the truth. It also takes an unwavering and unshakable faith. You will be led forward, if you have the courage to ask. In the end, with immortal guidance, you will find an altar of gold in the garden of prosperity.

I had become a Reiki Master shortly before I quit my job. I hadn't known much about this form of healing before taking classes with my best friend Beverly, but soon learned it was the perfect enhancement for my spiritual readings. Reiki is a Japanese technique for stress reduction and relaxation that also promotes healing. The word Reiki is made up of two Japanese words, "Rei" which means "God's Wisdom or the Higher Power" and "Ki" which is "life force energy." Because Reiki comes from God, it is really a spiritually guided life force energy that is effective in promoting inner peace and enhancing the quality of one's life. The ability to perform Reiki is passed on during an "attunement," or a ceremony of spirit, given by a Reiki Master and allows the student to tap into an unlimited supply of life force energy.

Attunements are both emotional and powerful for teacher and student as life force energy is being passed between them. As such, it is not uncommon to draw spiritual guides into these incredible ceremonies. I was blessed to see a spirit named Shikatu standing behind my teacher during my attunement. He spoke directly to me during this ceremony, inspiring me to walk my path, to stand in my truth, to be proud of who I was meant to be and what I was meant to do. His words inspired me to continue on my mission as a spiritual conduit. He told me not to be afraid of relaying the messages I received to my clients and to believe in their healing power. And, as is always the case with spiritual messages, his prophetic words were instrumental in giving me the courage to follow my new calling, to venture out on my own and hang up my sign announcing the opening of the "Hands Of Light Reiki Center."

As soon as I hung out that sign, my business flourished. I made the rent the next month and the next months after that. People came to my "Hands of Light Reiki Center" in Harmony, Rhode Island from all over New England. At the end of my first year in business, I had a mailing list of over 1,000 new clients, all built by word of mouth.

The business started to grow from there, and just kept on growing. It was at this juncture that I realized another important truth in my spiritual growth—that, with all that we receive, we should also give back.

I began to collect coats and books for a few youth shelters in the region, and as I put the word out, more and more people donated more and more coats and books. With their donations, came more clients and I soon needed a bigger space to accommodate my flourishing practice. But how was I going to accomplish this? I wrestled with the fear of the unknown once more and wondered aloud where I would get the means to finance my growing business. I prayed for the money to make this work and asked God to send me a sign that I would have everything I needed.

Sometimes it's the little things that can make the biggest impact. No sooner had I prayed for an answer, than I walked outside of my office to find sixteen cents lying on the ground before me. I stood back and laughed, thinking to myself that I was going to need a lot more than sixteen cents.

IT'S THE LITTLE THINGS THAT MAKE THE BIGGEST IMPACT

"You're joking," I said, quickly catching myself before I went any further with my comments. Knowing how God works, I quickly dismissed that thought. I stepped into that sixteen cents and said "thank you for the gift" as loud as I could, for I knew that would mean something. I took the sixteen cents, thanked it and blessed it, and put it in my pocket. Then I heard the words that today I repeat with conviction to so many of my clients.

Hold true to your faith every day and everything will be revealed in the right time.

I got into my car and continued on my way to the post office to check my mail. When I opened my post office box, I found inside a check for $50 from someone who had forgotten to pay me for a session. Then I arrived home and found another check for $50, for a reason I still don't know. I understood that this was a result of my sharing my gratitude for the sixteen cents and for having the faith to believe. That evening, I took that sixteen cents and placed it in a red envelope and put it in a desk drawer. I knew in my heart that I would have all the money I needed to finance the expansion of my business into the "Center for Inner Harmony."

A year later with my business virtually bursting at the seams, I was preparing to move to a larger location. As I was packing up my desk, I saw the small red envelope with the sixteen cents inside. I was overwhelmed with a feeling of gratitude for all the blessings I had received since I first saw those coins and thanked God, the spirits and the angels for all they had bestowed upon me. And wouldn't you know it, I made my way to the post office later that day and there in my mailbox was another check for $50.

I finally framed that sixteen cents in a velvet shadow box and keep it on my desk to remind me how important it is to have faith in your beliefs. I often carry it with me to presentations on prosperity to help inspire others, and then I send each participant home with their own sixteen cents. Sharing this story has proved a powerful gift for me as well as for those who hear it. Just sixteen cents and a dose of gratitude... can change your world.

THREE

MESSAGES OF HOPE

WHILE I WAS BUILDING my business, my personal life was falling apart. I was great at helping my clients receive the guidance they needed in their lives, but there were times when I needed to find my own guidance within.

A few nights before Christmas in 1992, I was in a department store shopping for presents for my daughter Kaitlin. My cart was overflowing with toys and games, as my heart should have been at this joyous time of year. But instead I was overwhelmed with sadness and immobilized by grief. Kaitlin's mother and I had decided to get a divorce a few months earlier. And the enormity of that decision hit me hard this night. It might have been compounded by memories of my own parents' divorce so many years before, when childhood tears soaked my pillow for nights on end.

As I thought about my daughter that fateful evening, I struggled with conflicting emotions about how it felt to be in her shoes, to be shuttled between two parents, and always certain to be missing one of them. And then I imagined how it must have felt for my father to leave his children behind, to live with an empty hole in his life and an ache in his heart. I wondered how he survived this loss. I was the father now, and although I had not walked out on my daughter as my father had walked out on me, I was racked with guilt. I left that cart filled with gifts in the middle of the aisle and I called to my angels to get me out of there, for I knew I did not have the strength to move on my own.

Somehow, I'm not quite sure how, I got myself out of that store and into my home. I don't remember driving my car, or even unlocking the door to my house. All I know is that I found myself in my third-floor apartment, sitting alone in the dark in my reading chair, crying, and having a conversation with myself as I called upon every blessed being I could think of. I couldn't understand what was happening to me, why I was experiencing so much heartache at Christmastime. The pain was truly unbearable.

As I sat there and prayed aloud, I noticed a small blue light in the corner of the pitch-black room. There were no lights on anywhere in my apartment but there was no mistaking the glow that emanated from the darkness. It was the color of the clearest, most beautiful blue sky you have ever seen and it was completely round. As if in an instant, the light got bigger and bigger until it encapsulated my entire apartment, bathing everything in brilliant blue, all the while nurturing and loving my tortured soul. It was larger than my house and greater than anything I had ever imagined.

It started out as a whisper. Then the whole room vibrated from darkness to light. Its energy broke through the silence like a symphony, growing louder and louder until it shattered the stillness with its triumphant beat. From this blue light, I soon realized that I was being given a spiritual transfusion by one of the most powerful archangels of all, Archangel Michael. He lifted me out of my pain and in that moment, I felt total freedom. I was reborn that night and had a knowing etched deep inside of me that there was no turning back from. I was exhilarated and exhausted as if I had just run a marathon.

Messages of comfort and healing can come to us when we need it most. To hear them, we need just to listen with all our heart. The messages may come as gentle whispers from angels, in the flutter of a butterfly that appears out of nowhere, a chime of bells where there are none, a sound, a scent or in the unmistakable knowing of that which you knew not before. In this case, it came to me as the purest of blue light and angelic energy, along with the most beautiful spiritually channeled words, which I call "My Song," a heavenly message that set the course for the next decade of my life.

I sit here in darkness. My spirit is alive. It lives deep within my soul. Oh, how such a spirit, desperate for life, desperate for resurrection. As I sit here listening to the music of my inner soul, the sounds are so distant. Within a crevice, a light has shone. Its edges only illuminating the music of soul. I feel the vibration, not listless, but bountiful. As I search, I see a shadow. It creates no tension. Its solitude is my peace. Its beauty is my life. The music of my soul is heard. As strong as the ocean wave, as quiet as a crisp, clear morning and as loving as a consoling touch. Oh, how I hear the music of my song.

Every letter, every word took on a life of its own. I remember that I was sitting there, sobbing and crying, feeling so grateful. In that moment, and there are many moments for all of us, all of the hands of heaven reached for me. So many of the people who had passed were there in that moment, thanking me for doing this. They were all encouraging me to follow my path, to step into my own truth, and not to fear the future. Even though at that time in my life I had but an ounce of faith, the spirits came and lifted me out of my depth, out of my demise.

This experience continued to affirm for me the existence of angels and divine energy in my life. It also restored my faith and my belief in myself. Where I had felt only fear and despair, I was now at peace. Where I had prayed for help and guidance, I was embraced by the tenderness of my angelic kindred spirit who touched my heart that day like no other. And while just moments before I was not ready to surrender to the angelic visions and encounters I experienced on a daily basis, I chose to move forward on my journey and profess to others that the visions that I so often saw were beyond possibility. They were unequivocally real.

That experience taught me that we only need to ask for the help and the power to walk through all circumstances of life. And when we do, we are blessed with unconditional love from a devoted band of spiritual entities who want nothing more than to see us succeed.

From that day forward, I began to receive more messages and see more visions than I had ever had before. I prayed that they were sent to me from a higher power and was reassured over and over again that these were angelic messages meant to bring peace and love not only to me but also to those who needed to hear them.

I began to receive my most intense messages in 1993. They were very clear and very profound. The messages were about humanity and the spirits who are always around guiding us on our path. They were also about God, not just about one God, but all the supreme beings, I learned that God, Jesus, Buddha, whoever anyone believed in, was all one body of light, one body of love.

One message in particular was repeated to me over and over again, and when I first received it in 1994, it was just what I needed to hear as I was trying to discover all aspects of myself. It is as relevant today as it was back then, and it can be applied to every one of us who needs encouragement to stand in our own truth.

It is time to look up to the skies, to the heavens and find your inner peace. Search within the refuge of your soul. Your voice will be heard. You will discover the beauty and truth of self. You must live in a world of both physical and spiritual, connected and intertwined as one. You must live together. You must coexist to achieve a state of oneness. You must live interdependently, loving, respectful. As you move toward the great light of peace and comfort, it is necessary to ignite a passion for those you meet. As destiny has no boundaries, neither does the coexistence of energy. It is in this passion and energy that we are able to move mountains and achieve goals.

DESTINY HAS NO BOUNDARIES

My angels are there to guide you. Can you feel them around you? Can you sense their presence? Your journey will reveal so many positive and unavoidable circumstances so that you can learn. I appreciate your dedication and devotion to the spirit inside, to the God in you. As we coexist, all will prevail. My angels speak to you with clarity and concise tones.

Sometimes I see that it is hard for you. Believe. You will hear the sound of angelic praises. I will send to you the softness of a caressing wind and the resonance of the harp. What do you see? Look from within. Use your spiritually gifted tools to see me and to see yourself. Release yourself and be free. You can discover your inner beauty. You can have peace. Once you have heard it for yourself, you will never look back. You are a capable soul. Take time to feel your spirit. Let the angelic light within immerse your soul.

It seemed as soon as I embraced one message, another powerful message would touch my heart.

Gather yourself. Apply yourself. The time is here and now for spiritual growth. Heed the message that comes before you. Evolve with your spiritual body. Release your pain. The angels speak directly to you. You have been called to heal. Use your hands and heart. Within you lay immense love, power and energy. Release all hurt and fears. Set it free and be the knowing force of love. Let go of which no longer needs to be. Let it all go to the heavens and it no longer belongs to you. Use your visions to help those that are misguided. Your spirit is strong. Stand tall. I have come before you. Your altar is filled with gold.

One of the messages that came right after that was:

Listen my child. I have sent a message. Follow the light. I am the only place to be. I have sent blessings and messages. There will be signs. There will be a sign that will clear the path.

Like so many of us when we are overwhelmed with life's challenges, I needed the reassurance that comes with every spiritual message. My world had come apart with my divorce and I was questioning everything. For months I tried to deny my faith, deny my spiritual awareness. I wanted to give up, to fade away, perhaps to die. But the spirits wouldn't let me give up. And thankfully, I never stopped listening.

EACH DAY BE REMINDED THAT YOU ARE A FORCE OF LOVE

Each day I was reminded that I am a force of love, that every aspect of me is a gift. It takes an incredible awareness to become all that we are meant to be. God sends his greatest messengers and disciples to each and every one of us, every single day. Some are in spirit; others are in the physical.

It was March 30, 1995 and I was at a friend's apartment. There were four of us there that night. Within minutes of my arrival, I began to feel the presence of angels and soon witnessed their arrival, becoming breathless as they soared above me. My hands started to quiver and my spirit seemed to join in their angelic movement. As I watched, I saw a pale blue presence with a golden hue glowing around its head and I knew immediately that I was being blessed by these heavenly spirits. There were four of them soaring weightlessly above the four of us. They brought comfort and love. One was wearing a garment of yellow, another was dressed in ivy, and beside them hovered a majestic angel of metallic silver. I was brought into a place of belief that there was no turning back from. It was incredible.

Many times after such experiences I would ask myself how I came to see such visions and to hear the personal messages meant for others. During those years of intense heartbreak, I found it very difficult to believe that I had been touched by angels who were sent by a higher spirit. Sometimes I felt incredibly foolish at the disbelief I felt, and so I wondered how I could expect others to believe if I felt unsettled. I knew from a very long time ago, that I was able to perceive and see "energy." We are all electrical bodies, so that made sense to me. But seeing angels and hearing spiritual messages, now those powers should be reserved for the chosen ones. What had I done in my life to deserve this honor?

I now know that we all share in this gift, that all of these angelic moments are all of ours to share. The messages are for all of humanity to hear as well. It is true that many of the messages are unique to the person for whom they are intended, but we can all receive healing from their meaning.

While the following message was directed to me so many years ago, I believe its words ring true for every one of us.

> *Your time is limited. Be strong. Move directly and straight forward. Follow my commands. It is in your words that I shall speak. It is in my truth that they shall listen. Be aware of forthcomings. Proceed with virtue. Prepare not for failure.*

Hearing such supportive and encouraging words was very healing for me, as I have found them to be for clients who come to me for readings. I know that everyone can hear the messages for themselves if only they listen to their own hearts and believe in the signs that are sent from above. So much of the wonder of life is that every morning brings a new sign. That's what the messages are.

The messages at first seemed to just appear, whether I heard them in my heart and my soul, or whether I saw them written in my head or on a piece of paper. Then, I began to feel the sensations of not being alone, as if I was being guided. Later I would find that behind the angels stood spirits whose presence engulfed the room; they seemed so enormous. Soon I could identify them by name, as if I had befriended them in the past. Now when they stand before me, I feel intense vibrations and then I hear the messages of hope they want to share with their loved ones.

My grandmother was one of the first "spirits" I ever encountered. She came to me three days after she passed, and visited me again many years later after I asked for her help in my prayers. This time she had come with a message for my mother, Terry, who had taken ill at the time. She was accompanied by angels who danced softly in a glowing light. She only stayed for a moment, whispering about her love for her daughter and me, and her new life in heaven.

"I must go forward, there's work to be done. Roland, it's light, it's love and warm as the sun."

She spoke softly, and off she went to the heavens, to home. Her visits made me understand that death was not an ending, simply another beginning. Through her, I also realized that time in heaven is not marked by minutes or hours, or days or even years, but by belief.

LOVE NEVER DIES

Though I had asked my grandmother for years and years to speak to me again, for her it was all in the same time. Time has no restrictions in heaven. It is a continuous flow of energy, never ending and never beginning. In heaven, time is just moments stranded together by love.

My messages and visions come to me throughout the day and night, no matter where I happen to be. Often, they come in answer to a prayer for help or guidance. But sometimes they manifest on their own, attesting to the protective help freely given by an unseen guardian angel.

TIME IS MOMENTS STRANDED TOGETHER BY LOVE

I remember one night when I was driving home in my car after working for 24 hours straight. It was in the middle of winter and I was as tired as tired could be. I got into my car after cleaning off all the snow and started driving. I came upon a stop sign and I felt as though I had been asleep at the wheel. I guess I was startled awake and I looked around to see hundreds of angels in my little car. I sat there and realized that I didn't have the strength to drive any further. Seconds later, I was home in my car, parked in my driveway. It was such a powerful experience. I said thank you quite loudly to the angels for bringing me home safely. But when I looked at them, I felt that they were extending gratitude to me for all the work that I do. I'll never forget that.

I will also never forget that in the midst of

chaos, confusion and doubt, if you hold a morsel of faith within, then you too will touch heaven as I did in my living room and in my car. I don't know how I made it from one place to another. I know I did and that's enough for me.

FOUR

THE CHALICE

As I grew more thankful for the gifts that had been bestowed upon me, I also understood that the messages I received were less and less about me personally and more about something much larger than I had ever imagined. The messages I received were for all of humanity to hear.

Now I was beginning to understand why the angels were showing their gratitude to me in the car that night. They were thanking me for letting go of my fears, for accepting what they shared, for believing in their universal love and for having the faith to go forward on my path. But most of all, they were thanking me for being the messenger and channeling their love to those who needed it most.

Gratitude is, by itself, a powerful spiritual gift that can move mountains. I've already spoken about the sixteen cents and how it changed my life. I was so grateful to receive those sixteen cents that I shouted my thank yous out loud to the heavens. In fact, I still have the sixteen cents. This priceless little sum, safeguarded in a frame on my desk, will always serve as a reminder of how very thankful I am to be where I am today. Often we may be too preoccupied to notice such a small gift, forgetting to extend our thanks to whomever gave it to us. But one of the most important things we can do is express our gratitude to the universe. Each time we do, it comes back to us one hundred times stronger. No matter how small the effort, acknowledging your gratitude makes a big difference.

That night so many years ago when I thanked the angels for bringing me home safely, I actually felt their gratitude towards me. There was no mistaking it; it was that compelling and it opened up a floodgate of messages that came so fast that I often enlisted the help of my friend Beverly to write them down as I imparted them to her. Both of us were astounded at both their frequency and their power. They revealed much of what many of us were feeling during these years and, with uncanny timing, they issued words of comfort to unburden our souls.

During slumber, I will reawaken your spirit and your faith. Be sensitive to yourself and others. In calamity, silence will be heard. The moment your heart finds sorrow, do not fear this; rejoice in the lesson it brings.

We all must climb mountains as we walk through life. I have scaled many myself. But after many years of practice, I know that I have never climbed one single mountain alone. I also understand that if there is a landslide or tremendous challenge, I will be outfitted with an armor of faith and knowing that I can withstand any turmoil, as each of you reading this book can.

Is your body tired? Then come to the water to refresh your energy. Is your mind tired? Then come to my house to reenergize your light. I am one with you. If you need help I am here.

AS YOU LOOK INTO THE EYES OF LOVE YOU CAN SEE THE SOUL

Each of us possesses the ability to see within our souls. A spiritual promise has been issued long ago that when looking into the eyes of love, you can see the soul. You can see its color, essence and energy.

The soul is housed in the heart, in the center of your physical body. The soul responds to love that is unconditional. It is filled with wonder and light. And it can help us in every moment of life.

Within each of you are the answers to behold. We have gently placed them within reach, within your heart. Just ask and doubt will be laid to rest. We make our presence known to you in many ways. Sometimes through touch, sight and sound, but in your dreams we do meet. Trust that I speak to your heart. Believe that I sit there with you, inspiring you every step of the way. Live and be free.

January 24, 1996 started out as an ordinary day for me. But as the evening progressed, I was reminded that no day is truly ever ordinary, when I suddenly felt an enormous angelic spirit encircle my body. I was compelled to look out the window. I saw a bright light streaming down from the clouds, looking like arms stretching from the night sky. Its edges were white and faded. Its center, bright and brilliant. I looked again and I could see hundreds of angels watching over me, watching over all of us. Hundreds of them soaring weightlessly through the night sky. I saw them in hues of light and beams of colors that marched through the night like that of a festive parade. Sea foam green to channel healing energy.

Light pale blue to channel communication. Off-white to channel freedom from the heaviness and burden of worry. Pale yellow to channel love to our emotions. Each was sent with a specific deed, duty and destiny for humanity. The angelic spiritual team had been sent to offer comfort, to heal our minds from self-implanted sorrow, to release our exhausted bodies and sanctify our darkened spirits. They ascend and descend with love and bring with them an amazing sense of relief that can truly set our souls free. I felt all of their gifts that night and know that you too can feel them if you believe.

Angels, mystical beings thought of in most religious philosophies, soar through dimensions of time and space around us, waiting to be called upon for service. They are messengers from God whose mission is to serve humanity in times of need. All you need to do is call them to you and the acquisition of spirit communication begins. They can hear your voice even in hushed tones and know what your heart needs. The bond between spirit and soul is reconnected at the instant a request is made. Their signal is often translucent. A quiver of energy passes right through you.

One or many may come, depending upon your faithfulness to them, to God, to the universal love that is in all things, and to yourself. They come with your blueprint transmitted through a veil of spiritual frequencies.

HEAVENLY LOVE IS PALPABLE

They cannot change what you experience, but they can offer support along your journey. I believe that we have all chosen our path before our life's journey begins; somewhere, somehow we have made an agreement. The choices we make are needed to complete our life's plan, but ultimately, they all lead to the same spiritual destination.

Often I am asked how I know that the angels or spirits are present. For me, it has become a crystal clear feeling inside and I have a peace so tranquil that I know I am being embraced. I am also never without faith and I often see Archangel Michael's energy shaded in light blue. Sometimes it's a feeling, a sensation or just a knowing that he is present, that they all are present. And his messages are very clear.

Trust. Today is a gift and that all our days are gifts. Trust. Know with certainty you have chosen the right path and are walking on the right path. The trust is in your soul. Be not afraid for today will bring you great joy. And that joy is also a true gift.

In the beginning, like some of you, I doubted the possibility that I could be touched by something so beautiful. Despite my daily encounters with angelic forces, it took me some time to surrender to their power completely. As time went on, I would experience visions with such beauty that I just wanted to stay in that realm of energy forever. But I knew that I needed to be in the physical so that I could profess to others that the visions were real. I soon had no fear.

Be not afraid for what comes today brings great joy. Your search for peace and tranquility is before you. You're on the right path to your life purpose. You are there. Keep working steadily and steadfast. Be mindfully connected to your path. Be still for a moment and see your treasures.

I remember one night when I had a message and vision so clear and unquestionably real, I could have reached out and taken it in my hand. I wasn't alone then, my friend Beverly was with me and a witness to an experience that branded my soul. I saw colors dance through the air and heard sounds that played like a mystical symphony in my mind and in my heart. I knew that this was another new beginning.

There standing in front of me, gathered as my own personal entourage of spiritual support, stood a band of angels and guides. I saw them. I heard them. I felt them. Gently they glided through the room, luminescent and mindful, transparent and solid, giving and nurturing, telling me what must be done next. I felt their presence as a reminder that we are loved and being watched over. Their love is not imagined and not a dream, but a reality that exists in me.

My vision extends beyond my angels to a man cloaked in a white robe. He speaks no words, but I hear him. He gazes into my soul and I am comforted and resilient once more. His light, a light that he has shone since the beginning, touches me now. I seem to understand and am overwhelmed at the same time. He appeared to me? I think for a moment, why me? Why am I blessed right now? Why am I presented this vision? For a moment I questioned many things, and then I felt his touch untangle my restlessness and fill the void with an expansive love.

TRUST WHAT IS WITHIN

In the quietness of that moment he reached out his hands to me and presented a gift. It looked like a cup. I'm told to drink from this cup. So I do what must be done. I drink its vibration. I feel its warmth flow through my veins, like water flowing through a river. I feel the joy instantly, as I am called to remember my sacredness. I am called to remember him and all those that have been summoned by God's love to be my support. I can feel the cup in my hands. My hands tingle, glow and radiate with what I am receiving...love. I am alive. This is no dream; I recall it in precise detail. It is an acceptance of what each of us is, if we believe.

I give to my dear friend Beverly, who kneels beside me, the same chalice that I am presented. She too feels its energy and is blessed, and comes to her own understanding, as it should be. The room is ignited with love, as it flows through us and around us. A thread of gold and purple light binds all of us together because it is the same opportunity that is presented to all of us. For those in the room and those beyond this place could possess the energy of the chalice. There is a moment of recognition and achievement that seems to be with me now. I know with certainty and clarity that the gift is in me, as it is in all of us.

As the chalice leaves my hands it becomes an angel, an angel for all, soaring, floating, light and free. I feel its love, everlasting and ever loving.

It is what we are.

It was a vision of the chalice, which I now use as my logo. It is a symbol of the eternal love of the highest of all universal powers, God, and it is there for every one of us should we have the courage to drink from it.

For over 15 years it has been my solace, my knowing, my rock, and my angel. It has been a reminder that the spark of divinity lives in me. That night would forever alter my consciousness and etch permanently upon me the spirit of love. It would give me knowledge and understanding that if I am to believe, then all is accessible to me.

That event occurred back in 1993, but it is still as real and powerful today as it was then. In fact, as I was writing this story down to include it on these pages, I received affirmation of what the chalice stands for—*it stands for humanity, for universal love and for the power that lies within each one of us. If you have the courage to drink from your chalice then all you ever dreamed of, believed in and wished for is yours.* God, as I understand his love, presents each of us with a chalice and encourages us to accept the gift that is placed within.

The message I received on November 7, 2007 reaffirmed that. It was accompanied by

what seemed like thousands of angels who filled
the room around me, all eager to stand behind
these words.

*Humanity can regain its consciousness. We
did not intend to go silent, but life has caused
us to slip away from each other. We have been
summoned to be together as one universal light.
Maybe we all have been silent too long.*

*Stand in your compassionate heart; it is
there inside you. You must take back the knowing
that you are one beacon of light, a ray of God's
breath, a candle burning brightly through the
darkness of night. It is who we all are. It is who
you are.*

*We, humanity, must remember that we have
chosen the journey we're on. As I said, it is what
we are. We are that symbol...the chalice...the
everlasting and ever loving light of God.*

God's voice echoed through my room. A
murmur fluttered through me. I could see what
I was meant to see, here and now, present and
alive. It was as loud and as soft as it could be,
all in the same moment. At that instant, my
whole being was elated and every part of me was
dancing again. I felt His, their hands, upon my
heart. I saw the golden aura of light streaming
through humanity, through you and me. I heard
what sounded like a symphony of angels and

trumpets cascading through every part of me...
and the message continued.

*I believe in you. I believe in you. I believe in
you. Trust that you will hear in the right moment
all that must be heard.*

We all search for clarity and understanding
and in so doing, we often turn to others for
answers. I have to tell you that the answers are
inside of you; you have the power to manifest
everything you need. Lots of times we make the
attempt to have a spiritual connection, only to give
up and doubt the possibility of that connection.
For some reason, many imagine that the heavenly
feeling they experienced was only a result of
wishful thinking. They wonder why God would
speak to them. The reality of divinity within is as
real as your own heart beating. You were meant to
hear your own messages, to know your own path,
to understand your own true essence. Have trust
and confidence in the words that are illuminated
within you. Trust that what you hear is what you
are supposed to hear.

One gift we have all been given from
heaven is having vision, not only for the present
moment, but also for the day that passed and the
day to come. I understand the power of now, of
being in the moment, but I also understand that
your insights can move you forward. Our holy

team has given us the insight to lead the world to a better place. Maybe some of the messages and stories you read in this book will inspire you to live each moment to the fullest so that your life will be beyond wonderful.

When you least expect it, your hands will tingle, your heart will feel serenity, and you too will drink from its vibration.

FIVE

MESSAGES FOR HUMANITY

AFTER THE DUST SETTLES, our emotions subside and the message is still present. I know that it's meant for many and not just one to hear the story that is being told. A message from father to son, from friend to friend, from child to mother, all hold extraordinary importance, as do the messages that validate and carry humanity forward. The stories that penetrate my heart and mind so deeply are the ones that need to find their rightful owners. I realize the story that is heard **FIND COMPASSION WITHIN** within me is for all of us, that we all can benefit from the sacred messages that are channeled, for it is a gift as beautiful as a rose. I have heard with such clarity that we must find compassion within ourselves, that the light of divinity is universal, and that we must become the community of support for each other. Messages like this sound like choirs of voices inside of me.

Back in the early nineties, my former wife would often tell me that I would get up in the middle of the night and have a conversation with someone, somehow, somewhere. She would go back to sleep and I would just be talking away, not always conscious of the exchange, but somehow knowing its magnitude. As a witness to my nightly encounters, she was the first person to truly encourage me to record my visions. She presented me with a cloth-bound diary to record the words and messages that came alive in the night. I agreed that the visions that filled my mind and soul needed to be recorded, almost to protect the legacy of the messages themselves. I started to document these messages feverishly in this diary, then on napkins at restaurants or scraps of paper just to keep their sacredness alive. During this time I was overcome with messages for humanity, messages that were meant to be shared. So I did what I have always done. I paid attention.

"The fuselage will fall from the sky," I said back in 1993 to my friend Joanne. I saw a vision of the New York City skyline. I saw smoke envelop the World Trade towers. I saw faces, so many faces staring back at me. "What should I do with this?" I asked. Joanne shrugged her shoulders clearly as confused as I was. Many of the visions and messages came too quickly to write down. Others demanded that I take note as if to preserve their integrity for some future consideration. One was dated September 11, 1999, at 7:00 PM.

Be still for a moment. Enlightenment must come so you can move forward. Gather your family to a safe place. I have told you to be ready. There will be a crazed attack in honor of the holy lands. It shall cause grief for so many. Fire and smoke shall cause outstanding devastation.

Eleven days later on September 22, 1999 at 8:15 AM, the message continued.

I have been with you for so many years. I have some very important information for you. I have told you in your dreams and awareness that great changes will come as you enter this new decade. It is critical to listen to your messages, to your inner voice. Many years ago, I offered a safe house. I shall do the same again. I love each and every one of you with the utmost sincerity and truth. You have grown strong, but seem to get lost on your path now and then. Stay strong and listen to the words of wisdom I have placed within you. Listen from your heart, not your ears. My children protect your flock. Such will be needed at a time of desperate reactions. I shall send more to you. Pray now.

The words I channeled on November 1,

1999 were equally prophetic.

There will be a change in the winds. The earth is unsettled, its nature no longer cleansed. The haven that it once was is no longer sanctified.

UNCONDITIONAL LOVE IS OUR ARMOR

You must become an instrument of safekeeping for its natural beauty. I look toward the next years. We need to follow rules of peace and tranquility. Go to your sacred grounds to speak to the spirit.

Messages that would change the way we see the world and how we would look at each other became the mantra in the early 90s. I heard that we will need to stand strong in the face of adversity, but we will survive with unconditional love as our armor. I made it my business to record and recite these sacred capsules of wisdom on paper and to my friends.

Time passed, messages came and went. Recordings were complete. Papers stacked up one on top of another. Then, in a flash, they were all gone. Words that had been secured on paper were stolen. There sitting on the floor of my car tucked secretly in a black briefcase were sacred writings. I had been compiling them literally for years for this book, reading them and rereading them often to feel their energy. They were gone. Vanished and never to return. I was beyond devastation. The tears flowed from me like that of a torrential rain spilling from my eyes and heart uncontrollably. It felt like a part of me was gone. I never saw those pieces of paper again. I had paid close attention to every detail spirit wanted me to share, and then in that one fateful night, they no longer existed. My friend Tim could not console me and could not grasp the enormity of this event. All he could do was comfort me with his generosity of heart. Messages that had been so delicately preserved...gone.

During the 90s and into the new millennium, before our world changed right before our eyes, I continued to receive messages that I did not fully comprehend at the time. Many poignantly foreshadowed an event I wished to block out, one too frightening to give credence to. Like my cherished writings, I sensed that the familiar was somehow to be taken from us, that things as we knew them were about to change.

What was I feeling at the time? I understood that we, as a body of people, would enter the upcoming decade with extraordinary mountains to climb. I sensed that the challenges ahead would shake us to our core, but not break us from our confidence. I knew that in the face of love and faith and in divine energy, we would not succumb to fear. I cannot tell you how many people shared these unsettled feelings. I received hundreds of phone calls from friends, clients and acquaintances, all seeking answers and reassurance to questions that suddenly loomed large in their thoughts. They asked if they had prayed enough, loved enough, given enough or were compassionate enough as if they were preparing for a judgment day of sorts.

My schedule took on more urgency as we neared the new millennium, and I appeared as a frequent guest on a local TV program. I was not alone in my quest to find solace and comfort for my clients in this changing world. My spiritually inclined friends were feeling this energy too. We talked often and prayed more, turned to each other for support and looked within and above for messages.

As dawn broke on the morning of January 1, 2000, I prayed for words and messages of guidance that could help guide me on my journey to help others. I sat quietly in my room and watched as a rainbow filled every corner.

Be grateful for today. You have witnessed a monumental event. Be steady on your path.

The unsettled energy will subside. Pray. Meditate. Heal. Send loving energy to someone in distress. Send love to humanity. Humanity needs you. Offer quiet assistance to someone in need. Love yourself. Give unconditionally. Allow love to seep into the pores of your heart then give some away. Feel the heartbeat of your inner child. Speak clearly. Listen clearly. Send healing energy to Mother Earth. Honor your spirit. Go back to your wholesome temple where you were created.

God, angels, higher power, angelic intervention, spiritual connections, whatever you want to call them, became more and more vibrant in my life in the weeks and months that followed, sending me messages that flowed from heaven like a river of energy into my hands and heart. They wanted to make themselves known to people everywhere. They wanted me to remind people that there is a universal light that shines, and that spiritual help and divine love is always there just for the asking.

On June 29, 2000, my soul was touched with these poetic words during a dream. I was compelled to write them down, to record them for some future moment.

I love my God for He never forsakes me. He gives me light to see. He gives me wisdom to teach. He gives me love to share. My God is a

*radiant beam of warm light that fills my heart.
My God speaks to all the people of the world.
None are left hungry. He fills all of us with the
freedom to experience His love.*

*By his virtue, He gives love unconditionally.
He embraces you when silence needs to be filtered
through. He lifts you when the walk seems so
tiring. He loves you when you feel alone. My God
is your God and your God and your God.*

*My God is in you, building a temple that
will house His love. My God lays the foundation
so His strength will permeate your temple. My
God gives you light to see the true palace.*

*My blessings are your blessings because
my God is your God and your God and your
God.*

These profound words made me realize
once again that there is truly only one God,
one light that shines directly upon the soul of
humanity, one universe that guides us to our
awakenings. I remembered in the quietness of
that morning that the human spirit is intertwined
with a gold thread of divine energy and we must
free ourselves from the patterns and thinking that
no longer support us in a loving way. If we chose
to experience that oneness, then we really were
living our true destined path. I felt the power,
and the empowerment of what God and divinity

are all about. I know and am reminded of how universal all of this is. With each breath that I take, somehow we breathe together. With each heartbeat, humanity beats as one. With the torch of love and faith within and palpable, then loving and respecting each other is possible. This is what God is. How amazing is it to be reminded of that in such a time of need?

I heard that the words channeled through my dream were words to be shared with humanity, so that they remember as I did. We must not forget that a divine light is in each of us and is one of love, support and joy. We must also respect that each of us experience this divine God light in

THERE IS A DIVINE LIGHT IN EACH OF US

many different ways, but it is one light that moves us. I knew as soon as I received this message that it was meant to be shared. There was a reason, bigger than I knew at the time that these words were entrusted to me. The vision became clear as soon as I asked for guidance in my prayers.

Send this message to people around the world so they can realign with the great spirit of God.

And that's just what I did. I sent this poetic verse to my friends and family, to churches and places of worship, to my client list and offered it on beautiful linen paper. I sent it to the spiritual officials of 26 organizations in countries worldwide, not just once, but twice, exactly a year apart, and prayed that they would be as open as I was and be as equally touched. I even sent it to the Pope on September 7, 2000.

To my surprise, people called me and thanked me for this message. Hundreds of people from all walks of life and all religions commented on it, connected with it and felt joy from it. For many it arrived just in the nick of time, when they needed confirmation of divine love. Through me, it was delivered. To my greater amazement, on September 28, 2000, three weeks to the day after I sent it, a letter arrived from the Vatican stating that the Holy Father wanted to thank me for my letter and poem. I am astounded that among the hundreds of letters the Pope must receive each month, that he not only read my letter but that he answered me virtually right away. I keep that letter as a reminder of how powerful faith is and how it can hold all of us up in times of need.

I know that God touched my heart in a special way when He sent me those words on that late June day. But as intuitive as I am, I never would have guessed their impact or how much they would be needed in the days to come.

A year later, the unthinkable happened. The days prior to September 11, 2001 my travels lead me to New York for presentations. There was a restlessness in the wind those days. As I recollect, many people were edgy and frustrated, but none could articulate where those feelings were coming from.

I arrived at my office around 9:20 AM that fateful morning because I had a 10:00 AM phone session with a woman from California. I had heard that something was going on in New York City from the TV, but no details were presented. I drove to my office wondering what had happened. Reports trickled slowly over my car radio that something was occurring in New York City, but nothing was confirmed. In the confines of my office, a flood of emotions nearly knocked me over. As I am remembering the events of that day for this book again my eyes well up with extreme emotion for those that lost their lives on that day.

I could see the destruction in my mind. It ravished me to my core, and the fear of those involved became so evident to me that it became my fear. I sat and prayed about this. I spoke to my spiritual team as I often did in meditation and prayer, to show me what needed to be seen. I sat down at my desk and felt compelled to sketch a portrait of a vision I had of a sinister looking man, with empty soul-less eyes and a scraggly beard. The lines in my drawing were dark and deep as if reflecting the anger and hatred inside of him. I also heard names of people, some recorded, some not. I felt like my healing center was crowded with souls trying to find their way back to their families.

Before me was an image of a man, his spirit was limp, his soul, heavy. I saw him in a haze of smoke and I told him he must proceed to the other side.

"It wasn't my fault. I'm sorry. I'm sorry. I'm sorry. I did everything I could."

Because of the way he was dressed I recognized him as one of the pilots of one of the downed planes. He grieved visibly for the lives that were taken with him before he crossed, at my urging, into the light.

"Go into the light," I said as I gently urged him on.

Behind him came a rush of souls who surrounded me in confusion and shock. They stood waiting to cross over unsure of what had just occurred. There were hundreds of them... and right by their side, hundreds upon hundreds of angels who bathed the room with a brilliant light.

I wasn't sure what to make of this so I called Tullia, my friend and mentor who lived and worked in Stamford, Connecticut. She told me that New York City was under attack and untold lives were lost. She too was ministering to hundreds of souls, telling them it was time to go home to heaven. I also spoke with Mrs. E., who, like Tullia, was assisting souls this early September morning. "Why did they come to us?" I asked Tullia. Souls seek out those of us who are open to spiritual communication and are sensitive to their energy she told me. They were drawn to us immediately as they too searched for answers and comfort that September morn. We were honored to help them on their journey and so grateful that we could show them the light.

We cancelled all of our appointments and spent the entire day helping souls cross over. We worked through our grief that day with the knowledge that the people who sacrificed their lives did so for the betterment of humanity. We were comforted by the fact they would be embraced with heavenly love, gratitude and peace for eternity. But we also knew that those remaining behind would face a new and difficult chapter in their lives without their loved ones. We felt their sorrow deeply.

I organized a healing support group that

evening, quickly inviting as many people as I could, opening up my center for those who needed to be here. At 7 PM, over 50 people had filled the chairs that were placed out in a circle. We came together to act as a conduit of loving energy to those in deep grief and pain. Every face that crossed our path on this horrible day was etched with sorrow. We prayed, meditated, cried, and collectively supported humanity. In our small group hands reached for each other, we became one circle of light, bound by compassion like never before. With our minds we embraced all of the families that were forced to see life so differently. Young wives, mothers, children and fathers, were forced to enter a place of terrific grief and pain, and all we could do was pray for them. You see I believe that when we hold positive energy, and channel beautiful thoughts, when we pray and meditate we send an invisible frequency of energy, and somehow whether conscious or not, the recipient is loved.

A few years later I was hosting a "Channeled Messages for the Soul" presentation for a group of 30 people. We had almost reached the end of the session when a spirit made his presence known to me.

"David's here," I said aloud. "David's here."

I made my way back to the far corner of a room where a woman sat quietly as if she didn't want to be noticed. But I had noticed her eyes perk up when I called out David's name.

I came closer to her and took her hand.

"David's here, your husband is here. He has a message for you. He tried calling you, you know. You were the last person he called from his office on September 11. He says he loves you and he made it over to the other side. He told you on that phone call what he saw that day from outside his window. He wants you to know that he is OK. He made it to the other side."

His wife didn't say anything to me, but her eyes spoke volumes as she nodded, acknowledging that last phone conversation with her husband. Then she sighed, almost with complete peace, as some of her pain was lifted by that message.

Not too long ago, I was doing a presentation when I was drawn to one of the women in the room. I had a message from a woman who had been gone for some six years now.

"Your sister is here," I told her as I made my way to her seat. "She had to help everybody get settled. She took charge and helped everyone around her, she says."

The woman in front of me started to cry.

"She was a stewardess on one of the planes," she explained. " I knew she would help everyone. That's just who she was."

I told her that I wanted to thank her sister. The energy in the room was palpable.

"I want to thank your sister, and all the thousands of people that passed away that day. They saved humanity shortly after that event," I said. "People started to look at each other again. They began to smile at one another again. They began to realize how important it is to live in the moment. They began to share their compassion without hesitation or doubt. I had seen people talking to each other with a kind, more gentle approach. Sadly, without the sacrifice of those people, we may have continued to go on as we did before, often too busy to take notice of the people and the precious life that was around us. The message that we must take away from this event is that those people who passed supported humanity in trying to find ourselves again. Your sister carried on that legacy of love and giving. And I thank her, and all the others, for their gifts."

As I reflect today on the event that changed the course of humanity, I recognize that through the mystery of life it is grief that binds one soul to another. We all have experienced loss, and often it is difficult to grasp the vastness of what that means. The grief becomes our advisor. It forces us to look within ourselves to find answers and to reconnect to the divine universal God that is within us and around us. As for the events of September 11, 2001, faces were cloaked in despair, hearts bled with sadness, and the present moment was so unclear. Together we stood strong and each day I privately honor those that passed on that fateful day in 2001.

IT IS

GRIEF

THAT BINDS

ONE SOUL

TO

ANOTHER

As I sat and thought about the sacrifice of life that day, an affirmation came to me, one which inspired me to continue with my work, especially important in the aftermath of that September morning.

I acknowledge, accept and trust my God. I choose to move forward with my angels. I choose to move forward with my own strength. I welcome the peace, love and joy that my divine God brings me. I do believe.

My journey as a channel is to share spiritual stories, to explore the realms beyond the physical, to create awareness, and to extinguish disbelief that nothing is there. As a channel, I serve as an intermediary between God and humanity, part of a ceaseless continuum of energy expressed from one dimension to another. Each of us has a link to this level of consciousness. In the days that preceded and followed September 11, my journey as a channel became more important than ever. The messages that I received helped me and I believe were meant to help others on their journey through this tragedy and life beyond it.

IT IS COMPASSION THAT BRINGS HEALING TO GRIEF

Humanity cannot maintain a level of hopelessness and fear. We must take strength in the knowledge that within, above and beyond is God, is universal love. And that heaven exists in all places. I have spent a lifetime listening to the sacredness of God's voice, through channeled messages, about the journey beyond this one. So many people carry such grief in their hearts, and, often because of that grief, have a misconception about what heaven is and where it exists.

What we perceive as death is the step that takes us to heaven. For heaven is not just a spiritual metaphor or a heavenly resort. It is a place where life continues. As we disengage from our physical bodies, we recognize that we have a spirit body that is full of life and choice. Think about this for a moment and make your own decision. It was the spirit, the essence, and the energy of your parted loved one, not the cloak of their physical expression, that you loved so dearly. We all feel so much pain and loss when a loved one passes, but the knowledge that heaven exists and that we will meet our loved ones again, hopefully, will bring you some comfort.

I have been privileged to pass on messages from those who departed suddenly on September 11 and on the battlefields of Iraq, from those who died in accidents, from those claimed by illness, age and more. Their messages resonate with one united truth: all is well. Some wise man once wrote "they have only slipped way for an interval, somewhere very near, to wait until you meet again." I know that is true.

For ever since my first vision of my departed grandmother and her angels and the many messages, visions and readings I had experienced with clients and friends in the years thereafter, I knew that life didn't stop when you take your last breath. It all begins more gloriously than ever in a very real place called heaven.

SIX

AND THEN THERE WAS HEAVEN

I'M STILL NOT SURE exactly how it happened. One moment I was participating in a Reiki demonstration with five fellow practitioners who were about to lay their healing hands over me and the next moment I was guided to look up by an angel's soothing whisper. I could see the light and the angels. I felt beneath my feet Mother Earth gently nudging me forward. I could feel the pulse of my soul as the light caressed every part of me. My feet danced with joy. My heart sang its song of love…and I knew. And then there was heaven…beyond, above and within me.

HEAVEN IS ABOVE, BEYOND AND WITHIN

Heaven is a place where angels sing constantly in harmony with each other. Heaven is a place where we journey to find our inner truth and it gently reminds us that we already knew, as we know right now. In heaven, there is a river of love that flows from God to the angels, to every ascended soul and to you. As you enter the world above you, you are greeted by so many that have known you. You're welcomed home.

Heaven is a place where peace and love exist. It is a place where love is unconditional, and it flows from every pore without restriction or limitation. It is a world of grandeur and glorious paths leading to the soul. It is a place where you feel your truth and empowerment. Often I am asked where heaven is. My reply is always the same. It is out there and within you all at the same time. And it is the most beautiful place that you could ever imagine.

I have been honored to glimpse the glories of heaven twice in my lifetime, many years apart. I was not close to death in either instance, I was very much alive.

Rather, I was granted an opportunity to witness what lies ahead and within each of us for all of us if we chose that path, a heavenly place, a divinely, holy, blissful sanctuary so glorious mere words cannot even begin to describe it.

Each experience occurred in seconds only, but for me, they were suspended in time. I began to drift out of my body, but I immediately knew that I was all right. My heart, as far as I knew, was beating. I thought I was just resting for a moment, quieting down, calming the tensions and easing the suffering I had been experiencing.

Within milliseconds of time, I began to float and soar in the air. I was slipping in and out of my body. The guardians and angels danced above me. It sort of felt like a dream but I could see the people in the room staring at my body. The first time I went to heaven, I saw my cousin Debbie's worried face as she looked down at me. She checked my pulse; I could see that. She recalls even today that I had but the faintest glimmer of a pulse and my body was cold to her touch, immediately reminding her of the touch of our deceased grandfather's body some 15 years before. I distinctly remember that moment too; it remains vivid and vibrant as if it happened minutes ago. There I was, weightless, unattached to life and invited up toward the heavens. My body lay on the floor for what seemed like hours. In fact, it was merely a few seconds, glimpses really, in spiritual time.

As I lay quietly, a ray of light shined down on me. I looked up to see a glistening white staircase. It looked as though it went for miles and miles, but I with bad vision could see the top of the stairs as my eyes adjusted. As I continued to look up, I could see the white light, a healing light brilliant beyond compare illuminating each step of the staircase.

I was invited to walk on, to move toward this heavenly domain. I could see so much ahead of me. I felt peace in a way that cannot be explained, only understood. As I walked forward, a shower of light poured upon me. I was more alive than I had ever been, a feeling that was recognizable once in my life as I gazed into eyes of my strawberry blonde haired little girl as she came into this world. I could see me there. My reflection was as I remembered. I was who I had always been.

I WAS WHO I HAD ALWAYS BEEN... LOVE

As you enter, you are greeted first by an assemblage of souls who have assisted you in life, then by your family and friends who departed before you. They seem to know that you're coming. There is a celebration as you are welcomed home.

I had been to heaven once before in the early 90s for an all-too-brief visit. I was invited to heaven again in 2000. Looking back now, in the aftermath of 9/11 and during the ministering I now do in my role as a spiritual healer, I realize that I was invited to experience heaven so that I could speak with unwavering conviction of the treasures that await there and of the loved ones we will see again. I was reminded that heaven is not only a place, but a feeling, an experience, an all encompassing gift for all to partake in.

At first, I could not focus my vision that clearly and I could not see what lay at the top of the staircase. But I could see that each step was going to bring me to a specific point of healing, a haven of healing that my soul needed. Each and every step illuminates God's love for all who walk this path. I could feel the warmth of that light. I felt it inside me and in places that I did not know that warmth survived, like in my fears, in my sadness and even in those hurtful times that haunted my memories. I realized at that very moment that I have always had the light inside of me. What an incredible feeling that was. I felt so blessed to know that I have the power to weather any storm on my faith and awareness alone.

I knew that this was the light that many see when they leave their body at the time of death. It is the light that you go into as you leave your physical body. It leads you to a realm of spiritual existence that is beyond your wildest imagination.

I knew that this was the beginning of the walk our loved ones take as they journey to heaven.

As you move into the light, your spirit takes on the lightness of air. You are no longer weighed down by the cares of life. The visions, sights and sounds left me breathless.

Each step offered healing. It was clear that some of us walk quickly and others walk slowly, depending on the amount of healing that is needed. I was moving slowly. I cried as I forgave the old hurts I carried with me, some created by myself, others caused by people in my life. I was overcome with joy as I had the chance to release that pain forever. We all will have the chance to heal all the wounds we choose to heal as we embark on the path to heaven, just as we can in our lives today.

THE LIGHT EMBRACED EVERY FIBER OF MY BEING

The light of the staircase embraced every fiber of my being. My heart felt no fear. As I looked up, I saw a hand reaching for me. It waved like a flag on a breezy day inviting me to walk on. This hand gently guided me and encouraged me to move up the staircase. I felt my heart trembling with excitement and joy. I continued to walk forward.

I placed my foot upon the first step and I

instantly felt the lightness within me. Nothing of pain existed anymore. I recall thinking that this was my walk home. As I moved up the stairs, I remember a feeling of complete peace and utter serenity. Every part of me emerged with that glorious light, and my once tattered spirit began to feel totally free.

The stairs were brilliantly light, but never blinding. As I had always believed, I instinctively and intuitively knew at that moment that there is purity and goodness in the world beyond. I climbed higher and higher, now with excitement and glee. My adventurous soul was emerging again. I was alive.

As I approached the top of the staircase, hundreds of hands reached for me, as if they were speaking to me directly. They sang to me a song that still reverberates within my soul. There was a sweetness that cannot be explained by words as the angels caressed every part of my spirit. I know that each of us, when we venture forward on this walk home, will too be loved and caressed, for they loved me so. God had placed his angels, the guardians and divine spirits on this heavenly walk, like road signs on a highway, to guide me to my destination.

I was not afraid. I was elated. Their hands spoke through touch. They blended with me.

My heart merged with theirs and fused a link of consciousness that words cannot express. As I looked ahead beyond the top of the staircase, I saw the most magnificent mesmerizing silver metallic angel. I knew that his job was to protect the heavenly door, the gateway to a paradise. I also knew that he was to oversee the healing process that had begun within me, as he does for all. I was touched deeply by his compassion and gentle love. Here at the gateway to paradise, you pray. You share your gratitude for life and you embrace the humility of divine love. Doesn't that sound like life here?

AT THE GATEWAY TO PARADISE YOU PRAY

I was encouraged to reach for the handle of the door. I reached for it with enthusiasm and courage. As I opened the door, one breath of life encapsulated me. It filled the chambers of my soul with an effervescence I never experienced before. This breath was God's voice, whispering and welcoming me home from my travels. I cried with intensity like never before. I knew He was there and I was there. The door prevented negative vibrations, thoughts, energies and old patterns from entering with me. I knew these emotions were not accepted here. I realized that the walk up the stairs was for healing the soul, mending the brokenness and releasing the suffering. The staircase is the sanctuary for the beloveds, a place of undeniable spiritual restoration. It offered the healing to me and I said yes. As we accept the healing, befriend the solidarity and remain faithful we walk towards a greater state of enlightenment and evolution.

As the door opened completely, I walked through the threshold and felt as if I was walking into another dimension. It was a place so familiar to me because I have always felt something like this inside of me. Walking through the door, I became breathless by the intense peace I felt inside. There were angels and spirits present, dancing around me in a celebratory mood. Departed loved ones were waiting for me. My grandmother was there. My wonderful friend Eileen was there communicating with me heart to heart, a form of heavenly exchange. Both she and my grandmother looked at me from a distance and didn't speak. They didn't have to. Their words magically touched my heart. In heaven there is a mutual respect channeled from one being to the next. The gentleness and kindness pours like that of a spring rain. We must allow our compassionate selves to be a constant companion in this life. It is what will sustain humanity.

There is life on the other side. They all came to me, those who knew me, those who loved me and those who cherished me. I saw them living. My life had not ended; it began on that staircase. I could see them communicating with each other, and most importantly, expressing love.

As I walked forward, the ground was as soft as cotton and hues of green cascaded through my visions. I was healed once more. Each step I took secured my healing even more. The air was warm and light. The sun was pale yellow, emanating with a warm glow. You could look straight in its core as if you were looking into the eyes of an old friend, like a friend lighting the path to clarity. I saw life in heaven. Heaven is not a place of stillness. It moves. It has freedom. It's life and it's love.

I felt all the people of the world were there, not just one group or one religion or even one belief. We come together there to finally celebrate love as it should be. As I moved forward, I saw two men dressed in golden white robes. The first man had darker skin than I did. His eyes were inviting, warm and comforting. Apparently he had always been my friend. He reassured me and comforted me. He looked into my soul and caused such an emotional freedom. He touched me as if he was my father. The other man, much older than anyone else who was present, wore his ageless wisdom like a crown, and made it known, without words, that this place exists for all. All of humanity and all those that honor love are welcomed here. Then He spoke.

You, my child, are on the right path.

Those words brought such peace. I was home.

I have led you here to see what exists beyond your physical reality. There is a world of unseen love and energy that when touched open doors to unimaginable truths. All of the answers are in your heart. We have created a heavenly link directly to the heart of you and to all. You must go on and help others to see their inner truth.

ALL OF THE ANSWERS ARE IN YOUR HEART

As the older man spoke again, his heart was solid as gold and his smile filled the air with sunshine. He said:

Wisdom belongs to those who believe in their truth. Words are spoken but become tainted without the deed.

I felt the two of them surround me with an indescribable love. They hugged my soul that night.

They stood before a castle adorned with white light and two golden doors. On each side of the entrance to the castle stood thousands of angels adorned in colors beyond the magnificence of blue skies, lush green grass and brilliant red roses, no color to be defined. Each man carried a golden staff. I heard that it was not my time to enter the castle.

Your mission in life is just beginning. You must help others see what cannot be seen with the physical eye. You are simply a catalyst, like so many others, to transmit love and knowledge to those in need. Honor all religious practices, cultural differences and spiritualities of the universe. You, like many others, are disciples. You are all disciples. It's time to go back now. Write the words and share the story.

All of a sudden, I see the door behind me. I now feel a stronger presence within me than when I started this journey. I look down the stairs, still bright and glistening with love. Now I realize that it is time to look down to Earth. The stairway still stretches her arms for many miles beyond my vision.

With each step, my light body becomes white and glowing and lighter still. I can still feel the touch of those angelic beings who gently massaged my heart with their wisdom. We are linked together with a golden thread and bound by love.

As I walked down the stairs, I could see others traveling up the stairs, their faces radiating unbridled happiness and awe. I desperately wanted to go in that direction, to go with them, but I knew it was not meant for me now.

I remember crying because I began to see the same beauty that I saw in heaven on earth. The stars were more brilliant than ever. Flowers radiated with more fragrance and colors unlike anything I remembered. When I finally placed my feet back on earth, I realized that the ground was as soft as the one in heaven and, in some unique way, they were the same.

The message about heaven has always been very clear to me. I realized with certitude that heaven can be found inside of me and was as equally certain that heaven exists out there. There entrenched within me is a well of peace and harmony that is as beautiful and radiant as what I experienced on that amazing journey up the staircase. I know without a doubt that each of us has the chance to access the heavenly domain that lives in our hearts.

I was sitting in a hotel conference room in Connecticut with a woman for a private session.

Instantly, I said to her "your father is here." I saw her smile inside and out glowing like that of a little girl waiting for daddy to come home. He has only one thing to say to you. "Don't worry honey, I see the staircase." She proceeded to tell me that when her father was passing on his final words were that he saw the staircase to the other side and that he wasn't afraid at all.

The heavenly part of you, of all of us, is alive and the expedition is just beginning.

SEVEN

THE BOOK OF LIFE

At the end of this chapter you will find the most profound pages of all. They reflect a vision I had on January 17, 2000 about the *Book of Life*, a magical tome blessed with the breath of God, blessed with infinity and blessed with universal oneness. A chronicle of who we are. The book is an elaborate collection of unbroken memories of a divine life, of questions answered and of sacred gems defining the journey of our existence. A record of a life lived...above, beyond and within.

In that vision, I was handed this book and immediately the pages opened to the center of the book as if the pages unfolded exactly to what was needed. They were blank. No words for me to see, nothing evident nothing existed, like nothing was ever present and nothing to learn from or to take refuge in. The wisdom of who I am was inscribed upon my soul, engraved delicately upon my heart, a place so utterly holy that the mere presence brings unrecognizable solace. As I placed my hands on the pages, I was touched so deeply it left me breathless. My eyes welled up with joy and I knew I found heaven. With my eyes closed I could see the white light glowing within me. I saw what others had seen in me, this vision no longer escapes me. I could see within myself; my essence became visible.

I FOUND MY VOICE INSIDE THE CONTEMPLATION OF MY QUIETNESS

My vision of the book reinforced the knowledge that I have about the spiritual book that is contained within each of us. I have lived my life attempting to discover all parts of myself. Through constant meditation and prayer I have found my voice inside the contemplation of my quietness. My *Book of Life*, like yours, is gently sitting within the compartment of love waiting for its revelation. If we have the courage to see the words of our *Book of Life*, then all aspects of us become understood. The book really has no pages or words, it's simply a metaphor for traveling deep within oneself, to commingle with God and all the sacred messages that are yours.

This is what I heard that night.

To my children, I give you the words so the eternal light will burn forever within you. I give you the courage to seek the substance of your soul. We will all stand by you as you embark forward. Sit in prayer and the silence will bring forth your book.

I created *And Then There Was Heaven* to share the extraordinary messages that have touched and opened my heart to a greater understanding that we are truly not alone, that love holds no boundaries and that it is as fluid as the sea. The messages in this book and within your own Book of Life come from God's love to you.

LIFE LIES SOMEWHERE BETWEEN EXTRAORDINARY AND MAJESTIC

I believe that life is beyond ordinary. It lies somewhere between extraordinary and majestic. It is not void of anything we need, but abundantly fulfilling, like the touch of a hand enfolded upon another. There is a world that is not seen, but is incredibly tangible. Love is that invisible entity that permeates our body, mind and spirit, always reminding us that the power and the faith are contained within our soul. Those that believe in something beyond themselves have the knowledge and comfort that they are never alone.

When it is time to leave the physical body, we will walk hand in hand with those we love. We will meet the souls who left before us, waiting under the threshold of the heavenly gateway. We will look back at our life, visit that blessed book and reconnect to the love we experienced in life. We will have a chance to heal the wounds, love the unloved, bathe in compassion, become a beacon for humanity and truly be light as it is intended to be. We will free ourselves from the ego and the emotion, and reunite with the life force of divinity. We will walk with the knowledge and power to choose the path that is best for us.

I am always amazed that if you focus your energy and attention, answers to questions seem to create a fortress of knowing inside you. I know that in the quiet moments of the day, you will be taken care of. Your book is brilliantly filled with words, phrases and messages that are yours. Find them inside.

I recognize that in our daily lives, stress can prohibit us from getting what we really need. In preparing yourself to experience the Sacred Pages of this book, approach it as you would any other divine connection or holy altar.

Start by clearing your intentions. Say the following affirmation quietly or aloud, whatever is most comfortable for you.

All I need is within me. I accept the glorious gift of my soul. I accept all that is there for me. I thank God for thee.

Light a white candle honoring the universal love that is present in all moments of time. Honor the Father, Mother, Creator and all that share love. Play gentle music to soothe your soul. Open the sacred blank pages of this book. Place your hands on the pages and keep them there for as long as you need. Allow yourself to unite with the holiness of who you are. Feel the light shine deeply within the core of your being and be peaceful. When this experience is complete, give thanks for all there is and all that you received. Spend some quiet time in reflection.

The pages that follow hold sacred energy. In writing this book, I knew that the words would hold beautiful vibrations and energy from days past and to present moments and beyond what tomorrow can offer. I placed one hand upon the book and my other hand upon my heart. I knew that with clear intentions, I could channel to you a sensation of loving peace and a oneness with all that exists. I knew that you could feel God.

As you place your hands upon these pages, the sacredness of times past bring words, phrases, parables and truths of your existence to this moment. All of the vibrations are channeled from a loving place beyond the clouds. As you embrace this moment, sacred energy blends with your soul vibration and the light illuminates all that you are. This is your light. Take a moment to be in your sacred sanctuary.

With your eyes closed, keep your hands there for as long as you need. Allow yourself to be encapsulated in the moment and embrace all the love that is channeled for you. As your hands remain in silent prayer upon the pages of the book, your soul merges with your heart and mind and you truly become one. Every time I visit this place, I am home.

These pages were intentionally left blank
for you to discover your own *Book of Life*.
Simply place your hands upon them and
feel their sacred energy.

Keep them here as long as you need
and embrace all the love
that is channeled for you.

EIGHT

MAKING THEIR WAY HOME

WHAT DOES IT MEAN TO DIE? I've never been comfortable with the word death because of its implication that the continuity of love ends, that in some way we don't continue beyond here and all that we've been no longer exists. It's absolutely true that the physical body does not survive beyond the experience of death, but the spirit, the soul, the essence is what goes on. Death is a word that has eluded some because of the fear that is derived from the unknown.

I believe with everything that I am, when my last breath looms nearby, I will walk into that moment joyfully knowing that I too will live on. A day will come for all of us when we least expect it, a knock on the door, a divine visitor standing patiently by knowing we must prepare and all of

BEHIND

ME

I WILL

SEE WHO

I WAS

the light shining around us suggesting that it is time to venture forward. Behind me I will see who

I was and in front of me, I will see who I will become. When I leave, I will learn, I will choose, I will grow and I will become even more of a compassionate vessel of love, as it is meant to be.

As I sit here at my desk wanting to alleviate your fears and dispel the notions that all is gone at death, I realize that all I can do is get you to the door of understanding, and from there you will have to decide what is best for you and what resonates with all of your life's teachings.

Spiritual music fills my office now with a sacred kindness and a familiar feeling overwhelms me. My heart is pounding hard, and my skin is tingling furiously. Out of nowhere, Brian stands before me. I see him in my mind, but I have never really seen him before. His heart is so big and he wants me to tell his mom, "I'm here. I'm really here." I say nothing to the only other person in my office, Ellie, my secretary. She has sat with me for years listening to the spiritual stories that have captivated one soul at a time, and there has been very little communication from him, other than brief messages channeled twice before. You see Ellie's son is here. He passed away unexpectedly many years ago. He appears like that of an ancient mystic channeling deep compassion for his mother. I seem to feel it everywhere and I am in awe of his tenderness. Through me, he confirms for his mother that he lives on, that he's with her and he is settled. Her eyes brim with tears as she announces that she had just talked about him last night, "how weird is that," she mutters under her breath. Wistfully she admits that she spends everyday thinking of him, looking at his picture, but not always saying his name. She tells me that her boy was an "old spirit." I agree, telling her that his compassion has journeyed with him to a holy place where it shines as bright as the sun. Brian says "that death is nothing to fear at all, that it is a beautiful experience if you choose to have it. You are always dressed in love."

IN FRONT OF ME I WILL SEE WHO I BECOME

Like Ellie's daily memories of her son, every thought we have of our loved ones becomes delicately etched in their energy, giving them the courage to move forward on their heavenly path. "I know your thoughts of me keep my spirit soaring," he says. "I love you so much Mom."

I close my eyes to imagine what his heavenly existence is like and I am shown pictures filled with colors and light, joyfulness and celebration. The sweet scent of wild roses fills the air just like it did when I was blessed with a treasured glimpse of heaven so many years ago. When you leave your body, you become as light as the air around you and the angelic guardians will sing songs that caress your soul. The angels gently awaken you from your physical slumber, reigniting your spirit and embracing you on the walk you must now make. Life, for this is truly what it is, will flow with unequalled ease then.

Years ago, as a caretaker for elderly patients at the nursing home where I worked, watching the demise of the physical body was a fairly common and expected occurrence. Along with seeing to my patients' comfort as they neared the end of their lives, my role as a nurse enabled me to support them as they transitioned to the other side. Each experience was incredibly moving, partly tinged with sadness at their passing, but also alive with the new energy that coursed through their bodies as they left their pain and suffering behind.

Today, in my role as a spiritual channel, I often get calls to minister to those who have but a short time to live, joining with their loved ones at their bedside. No matter how frequently I witness a beloved spirit leave its earthly body, I am always as awestruck as I was the very first time I watched a soul soar towards heaven.

I will never forget sitting with Celia, one of the first patients under my care, as she waited to make her way home. I was her nurse, friend and spiritual confidante. Her body was tired, and she longed to go. Too weak to talk, she could barely lift her voice above a whisper. Her legs could not bear even her frail weight. That day, as I looked around her room, I saw so many beautiful angels surround her bed. They filled the room with unconditional love, floating just above her, eager to guide, help, serve and embrace her at the moment that she was ready to leave this earth.

As she takes her last breaths, I see in her face the serenity of an angel. Her whispers widen. Words of gratitude seem to fill the void. I can hear her. She grabs my hand and I realize that it is time for her to walk home. The angels become her spiritual markers now, guiding her and holding her close. She stands for the first time in a long time, the wheelchair no longer her mode of transportation. She has wings now. Her

THE SPIRIT, THE SOUL, THE ESSENCE IS WHAT LIVES ON

body is transformed, youthful and free. Her eyes mesmerize me with merriment. In a twinkle of a moment, she is gone.

Our physical existence can end at any age and is especially heartbreaking when it involves a child. My memory of being called to the side of a teenager who was fighting an incurable illness has not diminished with time. David had been sick for years, but fought with a valiance that was truly beyond his young years. When I arrived at his house, his mother told me David was filled with fear and desperation. I could see it in the faces of his entire family, their eyes wet with tears as they shook my hand.

"He's in his room," his mother said in a shaky voice, cracked with sorrow. "It's too hard for him to leave his room now. Can you sit with him and help him understand that he is not alone?"

I nodded, gently consoling her that David most assuredly would not be alone on his new journey. I walked to his door, understanding that soon he would be free from all his physical pain. I could sense his growing anxiety as he walked around aimlessly and intensely within the confines of his small room. He instinctively knows that he has very little time left here on earth, I think to myself, but I can see his desire to live. I also know that he is conflicted and that he doesn't want to live this way any longer, as a prisoner in a slowly dying body.

David looks up at me and his grief overwhelms us both. He starts to cry. We communicate with our eyes. No words are spoken between us as we feel the connection of our souls. I understand that he knows that death is merely waiting for him to be ready.

I hold his emaciated hand, his frail fingers clenched in mine. His fear begins to diminish as I witness his pain and courage all in the same breath. He is so afraid of what the next minute holds for him, I can see that. I pray. Then we pray together. Within myself, I ask God for guidance. Almost as soon as I ask, I know that God will not let him down. When it's time, God will send his messengers to lead this young man to heaven.

I look up and see standing across the room the spirit of an elderly man with an infectious smile. It seems funny, I know he's old, but he looks so good. He's there to help his boy, he says. He speaks of the place where he has been residing. He tells me of heaven's gifts.

I share all of this with his grandson as his grandfather speaks to me in spirit. I tell his grandson how beautiful it is there and that his grandfather loves him so. I tell him the pain he has carried will no longer burden his spirit.

This brave young man visibly relaxes as he hears his grandfather's message. His breathing quiets as he lies down on his bed. He listens to the words channeled from grandfather to grandson and his expression becomes thoughtful.

"What will happen?" he asks with such a gentleness in his voice.

I tell him that a band of angels will come to escort his spirit home to the other side. Over there, I explain, reflection and renewal will begin.

OVER THERE, REFLECTION AND RENEWAL WILL BEGIN

"You will not have to carry your tattered body any more. Your physical healing will be complete."

"Your grandfather and so many others will come to greet you as you walk from place to place," I say. "Your spirit companions will caress your fearful heart and guide you to serenity."

He seems reassured for the moment. I continue to talk to him and tell him that he will always be able to communicate with his mother, and she, him.

"She will simply place her hand upon her heart and think of you. Your love for each other, and the love of those you have lost, is so deeply embedded within each of you that the memory of your life together fades not away but becomes even more beautiful. The love does not slip away into ether and will always reign high within your soul. Your face, your smile, your love, your light, your essence will always shine in her heart, and hers in yours. The love you have for each other will never, ever cease."

A smile skips lightly over his lips. His anxiety has eased ever so slightly. He wonders how his mother will be able to converse with him after he leaves so I continue to share with him my understanding of the heavenly communication that exists from one love to another.

His restless eyes are filled with tears again.

"How will I know when it's time?" he questions.

"On the day your angels come for you, they will sound their trumpets and an army of souls will lead you home. The path will be filled with so many wanting to nourish you and restore you. A light will shine on a step, and you will be encouraged to walk up. You will be loved, as you are right now. You will feel family and freedom as you feel right now. This will be the beginning of a wonderful new day for you."

His eyes met mine in a soul-to-soul conversation. A sense of peacefulness settled over him. Two weeks later, in the stillness of his room, this young man had the courage to go home. His pain was left behind as his spirit was rekindled

YOU ARE
SPIRIT
DRESSED
IN LOVE

with newfound joy. The love that is honored, experienced and respected here in life is indelibly imprinted in the clouds. That love is everlasting. Death chooses not to hold us back, but to reawaken the true spirit of love as a permanent soul memory, one that is retrievable upon thought and consciousness. As we leave this realm of understanding, we ascend towards freedom.

Death is not to be feared. When your time is upon you, the first step you take is for the renewal of your spirit. Each step encourages you to release old hurts, deeds and regrets. Healing begins as we move up the staircase to heaven. Our souls reunite there. And love waits for all who choose it.

Many years after David's passing, I received a message that affirmed the words I shared with him.

I have invited you to my home. It's a refuge for all that will come. The meadows of my home have glorious colors of yellow, gold and brown.

In the mountains of my home, the snowcap tops are as white as the glistening raindrops that fall from my sky. The grass of my home is like velour. Light green colors filled with healing energy. I have placed all these beautiful things in my home, around you, above you, beyond you and within you. For you.

While the pain we feel at the loss of someone cannot be diminished by words alone, the knowledge that our loved ones are safe in heaven can begin the healing process. A woman who lost both her sons just months apart sent me a letter not too long ago, recounting her own struggle with life after they were gone. She wrote that she fully expected to die from the pain and was upset when she realized she would not. It was only after she met with me and received her sons' messages, she says, that she felt like a mother once again. "In some strange way I feel even more connected to the boys now than when they were here on earth and that I have a purpose." She went on to tell me about the sign I told her she would find from her sons at her front door. "At 5 PM, the door bell rang and a delivery of Mother's Day flowers was left at the door. They were from my daughter-in-law who explained to my grandchildren that they were really from their dad and uncle because they couldn't send it themselves. I thought my heart would burst from happiness. It was the best Mother's Day gift I ever had. Lights flickered for two days and I just laughed and laughed. Thank you for giving me renewed peace and hope."

Carol, a grieving mother who had lost her young daughter named Liz, greeted me with breathless anticipation of what she hoped she would receive in her reading. Her face was joyful despite the telltale lines that revealed the trials of life. Her heart was filled with golden memories and she somehow knew that she was not alone. Her eyes swelled, showering her cheeks with tears. As I spoke, she remembered.

I sense the energy of an older woman in spirit standing next to her. She tells me she has a rested soul and she recounts for me the countless hours of help and comfort she received just before she passed. She speaks quietly. I begin to hear the unmistakable sweetness of the song, *Amazing Grace*. The sound fills my head with glorious pleasures. It's as if the angels are singing to me. In that moment, I experience an amazing sense of comfort. I share all of that with the woman who sits before me and she cries.

Now, a young girl comes into view, alive with divine energy, and stands next to the older woman. Her face is filled with innocence and her heart is tender and nurturing.

"I can see them," I tell the woman. "Your little girl and mother sit together on the other side."

Not yet into her teens, Liz wants me to tell her mother that she is not alone and that God took her by the hand that day. I begin to see in my mind this vibrant child whose physical life here ended, but who was just beginning her spiritual life. She speaks of the children she helps when they are getting ready to leave. She visits with them and takes them by the hand as God took hers.

My eyes are closed now and I see her smiling. She is playful, as children are. I tell her mother how happy I am that her daughter is there. As the impressions get stronger, I begin to cry. I can see this little girl, whose wings look like they are made of the finest silk. She takes the dying children home. To those departing, her face is familiar. Like an old friend coming to visit, she takes from them their fears and replaces it with enormous love.

As my vision becomes clearer, I see she takes them to the beach. I see many children, hundreds of them. I see their footprints imprinted on the sand. This little girl who left so long ago is now a messenger for God, guiding, healing and helping so many in that heavenly place.

Her mother cries and tells me that three days after her daughter passed away, she looked out her back window that opened onto the beach. There, standing on the beach with children she could not recognize, was her daughter Liz. They all stood together with their feet dug deeply into the sand. She told me they left their footprints as vivid reminders that what she had seen was real.

As hard as it is to lose a child through illness or an accident, suicide is devastating. As I prepared for a private session with a woman whom I had never met before, I envisioned a staircase, where, at the top, sat a boy as if frozen in time. I prayed about him and went on with my day. I headed out to the woman's house at the appointed time. She opened the door for me and I immediately saw the vision of a young man in spirit sitting at the top of the stairs, just as I had seen earlier in the day. I understood now that he had taken his own life some ten years earlier and his mother grieved as though it was yesterday. "He's so sorry," I said to the woman. "Your son is so sorry that he caused you so much pain."

"He can't go to the other side," I told her, "because he wants to make sure you are all right."

The woman told me that for 10 years she had hoped for a sign, a word, a whisper, a dream that he was all right. But nothing had come. She turned to me with a heavy heart and an even heavier conscience.

"It's going to be all right," I said as I asked her to trust me. I told her that we needed to take his hands and together walk him up the stairway to heaven.

"Close your eyes and take him by the hand," I instructed her. "Tell him, tell Steve, it's OK to go home now."

We were both crying as she did as I had asked. Together we joined hands with her son and walked him up the stairs in our hearts.

A SIGN,
A WORD,
A WHISPER,
A DREAM
ARE GIFTS
FROM
HEAVEN

"He will be able to move forward now and finish his journey" I told her, feeling sad and joyful at the same time. She understood that the three of us did what was needed that day to move on.

We met once more three years later. She told me that the emptiness that had ravaged her sleep for years after her son's passing was now filled with dreams of his triumphant journey into spirit. Her dreams became a constant reminder that their love is unbreakable, no longer shattered by the physical death. She admits her days are still sometimes long, but she is able to find peace more easily now.

So many of the people who come to me for readings have one question in mind. Did their loved one make it to heaven?

I am reminded of a private reading I had with a young woman in her early 20s. As she took her seat in my office, I saw someone I assumed to be her brother standing there and told her that he had come with a message.

"Oh my God, did he make his way home?" she whispered in her sorrowful voice as our session began. She couldn't wait another moment for the answer she had come looking for.

Off in the distance of my mind when she spoke, I heard a ukelele. It awakened a new understanding within me. I recognized the distinct strumming of this instrument and I knew.

"Your brother is entertaining the angels with the sound of his ukelele," I told her. "The instrument he so loved in life has never left his hand. He plays it with the knowledge of an old maestro from days past."

Her brother looked directly at me and smiled and I could feel his joy.

"He is playing for the angels," I said, "and he couldn't be happier."

In a blink of time, our hearts can be opened and we are united once again with those we love.

We are given the opportunity to be present with them. They walk in and out of our dreams, calling to us. They whisper in our ears in the middle of the night. You may awaken and desperately look for them, only to find that they aren't there. Grief overwhelms you at that moment and you go back to sleep. In the morning you remember that something beautiful happened in your dreams. Was it real you wonder?

If you wake up with a memory so vivid that you find it hard to believe that it didn't actually happen, it could very likely have been a spiritual visit from a departed loved one, presenting you with an undeniable sign that love is everlasting. I know from the very depths of my soul that the separation from life to death does not keep us apart. No love is ever lost.

I share these stories with you because messages often come in the most unexpected ways. The sound of a ukelele, a footprint in the sand, a scent, a shiver of energy, a dream—all can trigger a beloved memory. Remain open hearted and ready to experience their love. They are truly there whenever you need them if you listen closely and believe in the power of your love.

NINE

CHANNELED MESSAGES FOR THE SOUL

EVERY DAY BRINGS A NEW STORY, and with it, a new affirmation of heaven and life beyond. All you need to do is listen. That's what I do. I start each day with a prayer and I ask the universe what messages I need to share. During my prayers, I am routinely given fragmented communications that I write down. A name, a date, a phrase, a picture. By themselves, the messages don't hold any meaning for me. Only the intended recipient holds the key to their meaning.

Experience has taught me that these channeled words will bring peace to the person who is waiting to hear them. I diligently jot all of them down on pieces of paper that I bring with me to every session. I've been carrying some of the messages around with me for years; the papers on which they are written are beginning to tear at the corners. No matter how long ago I wrote them down, I know that I will be able to deliver them to the right person in due time even though I never know who or when. But I do know that all of the messages are sacred and are intended to heal the soul. They may not be exactly what the person wants to know. But they are exactly what they need to hear.

Whether I am meeting with one person for a private session or groups of 30 or more for a large presentation, I begin with an introduction and a disclaimer. I am here, I tell them, not to convince them that there is another side, but rather to pass along the messages. My job is simply to listen, I explain, and to share what I hear. Don't put your faith in me I advise. I didn't go to a special medium-ship school and I don't have a degree in this. My training started the day my grandmother visited me when I was just 10 years old. Like me, each of you has the power to hear the messages and feel the love from the other side. All you have to do is believe in yourself.

I also admit that I am not sure how the session will go. "Let's see what happens" has become my standard opener, as I acknowledge the unscripted events of the moments that are sure to follow.

Unfailingly, just as soon as I get started, the voices of spirit begin. I hear them as if they are standing right there next to me. They all talk at once, so anxious are they to send a message to someone in the room—a psychiatrist would have a field day with me, I joke. As you can imagine, it can be pretty hard for me to think of what I was about to say next, and equally hard to stay on course with any prepared remarks. One by one, I scan the faces in the room as I find the people who the messages are for.

BELIEVE

IN

YOURSELF

"Who has a badge with them?" I ask at a presentation I am giving in Stamford, Connecticut, "a fireman's badge?" A woman in the third row reaches into her pocket and hands me the badge. "Your brother's here," I tell her. "Joe's here. That was his badge," I say. "He wants me to tell you that he is fine. He was trapped in the fire and he couldn't get out of the building. But he died doing the job he loved and he's fine now." The woman starts to sob. Her brother was a fireman who was killed fighting a fire in a building in Stamford some months earlier. At that moment I remember the message I had written down early in the morning about a fire. I rifle through the notes that I had brought with me and find what I am looking for. It is a sketch I drew of a tall building engulfed by flames. At the top of the drawing, I had written the words "Stamford and Joe." I give it to Joe's sister during the presentation. I tell her that her brother is safely on the other side and that she too is going to be all right.

"I have to talk about the little girl," I say as I began a presentation in Wilton, Connecticut. "She's three years old. Does anyone know anything about this little girl?" No one answers so I move on to a group of teenagers sitting in the back of the room. I also have to talk about the boy in the car accident. No one speaks. I break the silence as I hear a message intended for the young people who sit together.

"Your friend's here. He says to tell you that he's all right. He couldn't make it out. He was going too fast." The words flow quickly. "He still looks great," he says. "He's lookin' good and he's wearing all white." The boys laugh knowingly at the thought of their buddy all dressed in white. It becomes more apparent that their friend has a lot to say tonight as I hear special messages meant for each one of them. I move among them as I tell them what I hear.

"Eric, don't throw away your plans," I say to one of the boys who listens intently to the words of advice he receives. "Don't stop. Keep working on them." I can see these words resonate with Eric and just know that his departed friend had been a pivotal force among this group.

"Mark, did you bring a picture?" I ask another boy who almost immediately pulls out a picture from his jacket and shows it to me. "He says that he was much better looking than that. Is that the best you could come up with?" Their mood lightens.

"John," I address a boy who looks straight ahead, as if he is afraid to hope that his friend will acknowledge him. "John," I say again, louder this time to jolt him into the magic of the moment. "He hasn't forgotten about you. He knows you want to see him again. You asked that in the drive over here and he heard you. You will see him again," I promise him. "In January of 2008, he will make his presence known to you. He believes in you so don't be doubting yourself," he says. The boys smile again when I mimic a macho stance that he must have assumed as part of his distinctive personality. In so doing, I validate his presence to those who knew him in the prime of his life.

Everyone in the room was witness to the healing that began in those moments. The young man who had passed in the car accident made an undeniable connection that night with his friends and was able to keep his love alive even though he was no longer here in the physical. Equally compelling was the fact that teenage boys are not usually regulars at my group sessions. I knew there was something larger at work to have brought them here and was glad they were able to find some peace in their grief. No matter who the message is for, we all benefit from the experience. The moment it begins, it awakens our compassion for a soul that is suffering.

I start to move away but the boy wasn't finished talking yet. It is virtually impossible for me to repress channeled messages once they start. I am directed to a man who was sitting behind the teenagers, leaning against the wall. Next to him were two young girls who I instinctively knew were sisters of the boy who was in the car accident.

"Bill. Dad. Bill." I switch between his name and the name his son calls him. "Your boy's here," I say loudly. "Your boy wants you to know that he loves you so much. He is sorry that he had to go. He couldn't get out of it. He's sorry his passing has caused everyone so much pain. Tell my dad that I'm OK. I'm settled here."

"Mandy, everything will be all right," I tell his sister, relaying a message from her older brother. "You worry too much. I love you. Take care of your little sister. She needs you."

As I relate the messages from this boy to his father and his two sisters, I remember a note I had brought with me. I flip through the written messages and pull out one that has a picture of a winding road, the name Bill, and the words "I'm sorry. It happened too fast. I love you." I fold it in half and give it to his father to read later. I know he will find comfort from it.

"I still have to talk about the little girl," I say to the group. No one seems to understand this message until I speak to a young woman with a sad expression on her face. "What is your question?" I intuitively ask her.

"I would like to know about my mother," she answers.

I ask her how her mother died, but she tells me she doesn't know. I assure her that her mother did not commit suicide nor was she murdered. "Everything just went dark for her. She wasn't afraid," I said. "She is talking about her little girl," I tell the group. "She was only three years old," she says. I ask the young woman how old she was when she last saw her mother.

"Three," she says.

"You're the little girl I am supposed to talk about," I say excitedly. "Your mother was not murdered," I repeat, "and she did not commit suicide. Do you understand that? She was here one minute, and gone the next. She never meant to leave you. She loved you."

The young woman wasn't sure what to

make of this message. I realized that she had been abandoned by her mother at a young age and never knew why. I could tell that she was somewhat skeptical about what she had heard, but was also interested in learning more.

"What is your name please?' I asked her.

"Rain," she replied.

"I know why you came here tonight," I said as I ran to the table in front of the room where I kept the written messages. "You came to get a message from your mother." I stopped talking and immediately found what I was looking for. "I've been waiting for you. I have a message for you," I said as I showed her a piece of paper I had written on months before. There

I'M ALWAYS was a picture of a rainbow on it along with lots of hand-drawn

THERE raindrops. The words, "three years old" and "little girl" were there,

AND I'LL as were heart-felt sentiments that

ALWAYS were clearly meant for the young woman who sat before me. "I

LOVE YOU have always loved you. I wasn't afraid that night. Something happened, a distraction, and then I was gone. I am always with you and will never leave you. I am going to send you the most beautiful red rose you've ever seen. Look for it and believe. Never forget this night. I love you."

There wasn't a dry eye in the room after that.

Poignant stories and messages like these are commonly punctuated with lighter moments, attesting to the different needs of the people who come to these channeled message sessions.

"Does someone have a brand new car parked out in the back parking lot?" I ask. "It's a beautiful green color. I think it's a Buick." A young man in the back smiles. "Your father is standing behind you now. He loves that car. He's says 'good for you son. You earned it.'" His son beams as he hears his father's message.

"Your grandfather's here," I say to a man named Mike. "He's a little bit on the grumpy side," I tell him as the room erupts with laughter. I explain that I have to tell it like it is; there are no filters here. In fact, I see their departed loved ones as plainly as I see the people in front of me, with clarity and details that they were familiar with in life. And yes, they can still be funny. "He's making faces and he is saying that this is not his thing. He doesn't want you to worry about all the crazy things you get in your head. And he doesn't want to talk about the last day. He made it to heaven, he says, and he's with your father."

Many people who attend my sessions bring keepsakes with them to remind them of their loved ones. It could be anything that holds special meaning for them, a ring, a locket, a photograph. It is a connection for them, one that they feel forever binds them to their loved one. I know they are already bound together by their love alone.

"Did you bring a book with you?" I asked a woman with a big purse. "May I see it please?" As she was rummaging through her bag, I tell her that she will find a sign in the Psalms. "Your great aunt loved that book," I said. "She has a message for you in the book."

The woman finally found the book and handed it to me. There was a bookmark in it, opening to Psalm 24. "Your aunt tried so hard to stay," I told her. "She liked taking care of all of you and she is continuing to take care of you from above."

Her aunt, I learned later, was 95 years old when she passed, and had taken on the role of mother for her extended family. Her grandniece held that book to her heart and I knew she would understand her aunt's message contained within.

"Is there someone you are missing?" I ask a young woman who sat with her sister at the end table in an intimate group presentation. I had given her several messages during the evening session but still she looked confused. "I wanted to hear from my father," she said with a lump in her voice. "How long has he been gone?" I asked her, for I was not getting a message from him. She told me he had passed away five months earlier, in October of 2007.

I took a minute to focus on her father and saw that he was still in a place of healing, a step we will all take on our way to heaven. "He knows you were there with him during those last days I tell her. He felt you stroking his right arm three days before he passed. He had a massive heart attack."

The girls gasped as I continued with the messages and asked them if they had brought something grey with them. One of them reached into her bag and pulled out a grey tee shirt. "I know about him, " I said as I remembered a message I had received weeks before this session. I had written the words "grey flannel" and a note about his favorite shirt, along with a date, November 28, 2007. "Well it's not a grey flannel shirt," I noted as I looked at the shirt the woman carried with her. "But it's close enough," I laughed. With those words, the two sisters began to sob loudly and one of them pulled a bottle of "Grey Flannel" cologne from her bag. "He wore it all the time," she explained. "Grey Flannel was his signature cologne."

We talked later about the significance of the date I had put on the same piece of paper. Your father sent you a sign that day I told the woman's sister. She remembered that moment as if it happened yesterday, telling me that she had been shopping for Christmas presents at the mall right after Thanksgiving and passed by a man who was wearing Grey Flannel. The scent was so distinctive she immediately thought of her father. "That was a message from him that he was alright," I said. She understood it completely.

"Who has lost their dog?" I ask. "A woman raises her hand. "Dogs make it to heaven too. You did all the things that you were supposed to and you gave him lots of love. His legs didn't work anymore. He's running free now."

As powerful as these group sessions are, private readings can be even more life changing. Clients schedule personal readings with me for all kinds of reasons. Some hope for a glimpse of the future. Will I ever find my soul mate? Should I change jobs? When will the financial burden be lifted from my life? Where do you see me living next year? Others want to hear that their relatives will be all right. Will my son get married soon? How is my mother's health? Is my sister going to sell her house? I am not a fortune teller and I can't predict the future. There is always an element of choice that affects a person's journey on earth. As I remind my clients, I'm just the guy who passes along the messages. I tell them what I see and what they are meant to hear. I cannot predict or control what the session brings.

I have channeled messages to thousands of clients. Some stories stay with me, as powerful today as they were when I first experienced them. Others are triggered by a similar story, a random discussion with a friend or client—or a vision or a sign I told them they should look for in the days to come. It is almost impossible for me to remember all the stories I share in those intensely personal moments, for each was meant for them alone to cherish as they moved forward on their journey.

Writing this book has brought many experiences back to me, some in the form of chance meetings with old clients, others volunteered by friends who thought they would be inspiring for others to hear. I am honored to share several of them here, recounted by my clients as gentle reminders of the healing powers they manifest.

Cynthia drove up to Harmony, Rhode Island from Connecticut to meet with me for a private reading in my office.

"Cynthia, you are being touched by angels," I said when our next session began. "Your father is here. He says he's sorry that you felt he didn't love you. He just didn't know how to show it. He wasn't brought up that way. He says he's always loved you, Sam."

Her father had passed away 22 years ago, in 1978. She hadn't heard his nickname for her for many years before that. He had affectionately called her Sam due to her eagerness in helping him do chores usually relegated to the 'man' in the house when she was a little girl.

"Your father is always there for you and he is watching over you. He's very proud of you," I told her in that reading. "He wants me to tell you that. He knows he never told you that when he was alive. He was uncomfortable with displaying his emotions. He says that was him you saw in the airport that night. He knows no one believed you. He says that whenever you need his help, all you need to do is reach out and he'll be there."

Another spirit made her presence known during our visit. "There's a woman in the back of the room, Cynthia. She was someone who you used to laugh and have a lot of fun with. You would go out and the night would slip away before you knew it."

Cynthia didn't seem to know the person I was talking about.

"She's telling me that the words you whispered in her ear gave her comfort. You whispered, ' don't be afraid. It's OK to go. We all love you.'"

Cynthia looked surprised as she remembered the exact words she had shared with Dottie who passed away from cancer in 1991.

"She understood why you could not make it to the hospital to say good-bye and she says that it was OK. She knew you were by her side at her daughter's house every day before she went to the hospital. She was always concerned with the long drive you made from Connecticut after you got off work to be with her. She also wanted to apologize and to let you know that it was the medicine talking when she would tell you to get out of her room as you were sitting by her bed. She hoped you weren't hurt by those words."

I laughed as Dottie added "thank you for letting me have my cigarette and scotch when I visited you in New Canaan after I got sick. My family wouldn't let me near them anymore. You know how I loved my scotch. I am grateful to you for that too."

Cynthia smiled at the memory.

During the channeling of messages I often sense and witness the benefit of my work in full force. Often a light of compassion is lit, and the spark of humanity begins to light the darkened path with hope. A hand reaches for someone, a tissue is passed, love is shared and the audience is one. Somehow the reaction of the recipient of the channeled message intertwines with what we all are feeling in that moment. There is a camaraderie in that moment as we all grieve at the loss someone else is feeling.

ONCE A LIGHT OF COMPASSION IS LIT, HOPE IS RESTORED

I did a radio show and a caller started to tell me "my daughter's gone, my husband's gone..." and then I felt the need to stop her. I told her that her daughter sends her the most beautiful birds in her backyard to the right of the house. She screamed with obvious jubilation, saying that she witnessed the presence of her daughter's sign, her daughter's love. She said with such pride "she did that yesterday."

The next caller was another woman who told me that was the most beautiful story that she had ever heard. The radio host was moved to near emotion and I was left breathless. In truth, the ability to communicate with our departed loved ones and the reality of heaven is greater than any other journey known.

Cheryl was surprised by the message she received in a personal reading with me during a spiritual wellness event held at a Connecticut hotel. "There are two spirits with you," she remembers me saying. "There are two gentlemen with you, one is a lot older than the other. It sounds funny, but they both have the same names. They want you to tell Rick, the person you came to this event with today, that they are here for him and support him in his new venture." Cheryl didn't know who they were she told me, but she told me she would pass it along to her friend Rick whom she only recently had begun to date. Later, she found out that Rick's father and stepbrother, who he had been very close to and who had both passed over, were named Fred Warren and Warren Fred. Rick was delighted with this message as it gave him the added support and confidence he needed to pursue his new business venture.

Words of encouragement from the other side are offered just when a person needs it most. We only need to be open to the message to feel its loving power. My clients often find their messages to be amazing in their accuracy and timing. I always find them amazing in every way.

4191. I had written these numbers on a purple piece of paper along with an American flag, and a message related to the Iraq War. I did not know what to make of them yet but I knew that I had to carry them with me until they found the rightful owner.

I was doing a presentation a few nights later when I felt the spirit of a young man with an American flag standing next to a woman in the group. As I went over to her, I had a vision of a dirt road and an army jeep driving along it. I heard gunfire and saw clouds of dust. I looked closer and saw four men riding in that jeep. Then in an instant, I watched as three angels came down from the sky and carried three limp bodies of young men away. Then there was a horrific explosion.

The woman sat in front of me not daring to speak, move or even breathe. I continued to describe what I was feeling.

"He left before the jeep hit the land mine," I said. "Your son did not feel any pain. He was already gone. He was in the arms of an angel who protected him from the horror of those last moments. He says to tell you that he's all right now."

As I spoke with her, I remembered the message that was recorded days before, 4191. I told her the numbers meant something and were from her son. Neither of us knew why.

A few months later, the woman contacted

me. She said that after the presentation she had flown out to Missouri, bringing the paper with her. During that trip, she visited the soldier, the only survivor of that awful day, who was driving in the jeep when her son was killed. When she met with him, she told him about the messages and thanked him for his friendship with her son. She showed him the piece of paper with the number 4191 on it. His face paled, as did hers when she discovered that the jeep they were driving in on that fateful day was identified as jeep number 4191.

Each of us can benefit by the messages that are channeled from heaven, for while their stories may be very personal, their truths are universal. In times of tragedy especially, it is comforting to know that we have a god who loves us. He is always watching over us. God cannot change the will of man, but he can release the soul to spare us from unimaginable pain.

Nancy sat in the front pew of the small Greenwich church where I was giving a presentation on gratitude. "I'm not here to share any messages tonight," I said to the crowd of 100. "I'm here to talk about the power of gratitude. Tonight is about thanking the universe and thanking each other for all the gifts we receive everyday."

I am interrupted by a spirit who wants to

get a message to Nancy. "Sorry," I say to him. "I'm not going to share any personal messages tonight." I continue with my presentation, determined to stick with my planned agenda.

BIRDS, BUTTERFLIES AND PENNIES ARE GIFTS FROM HEAVEN

If there is one thing I can be sure of from all my years as a spiritual channel, you must always expect the unexpected. When spirit speaks, you have to listen. The spirit of this man would not take no for an answer. His persistence made me smile inside. No sooner had I told him that this wasn't the time for his message than I found myself almost running over to Nancy in front of the church.

I reached for her hand and found myself telling her not to let go of my hand.

"There is a gentleman here who is very insistent that I speak to you," I said to her, before the channeled messages came flowing out as if they had been held back by a floodgate. "I love you," he says. "I love you. Don't let go of my hand. I've been trying to send you messages," he says, "but I know how you get." He says you were the light of his life and he loved to make you laugh. He knows you talk to him every night. He hears you, Nancy. He loved to hold your hand, he says. "Don't let go of my hand," he says. He is waiting for you he says. "Don't worry so much," he says. Everything will be all right. I love you."

The love we share with those closest to us is eternal and never dies. I have known this since I was a little boy and it is continually reaffirmed during readings, presentations and channeled messages from above. Spiritual messages are meant to inspire healing. They are divinely guided for this purpose and they are filled with love. If you truly believe, messages have the power to replace pain and suffering with faith, hope and understanding.

TEN

I BELIEVE

THE POWER OF FRIENDSHIP was never so clear to me until the spring of 2007. I answered the phone as usual. "Roland Comtois speaking." The person on the other end could barely speak. Her words were scarcely audible and her breath was shaken into pieces. Grief had taken her voice from her. Her pain was measured by sadness that rang through my heart at her words. "Sue is gone," she announced to my disbelief.

That phone call was the beginning of a time of great sorrow for me. What I had preached to so many would now become my personal mantra. Sue was one of my favorite students, a quick learner with a bright smile that radiated her enthusiasm to everyone in the class. She had earned her Reiki Master Certificate under my tutelage, and was eager to share her gift with the world. Now she was gone, suddenly passing away in the prime of her life. She was just 42 years old.

Destiny had led me to this moment to teach

me another lesson. At her service, Sue's family and friends gathered together to celebrate her life.

DESTINY LEADS US TO MOMENTS OF GROWING

As I walked through the funeral home to greet them it hit me that I had been an important part of Sue's life. Remnants of that connection existed in every part of the room, from the Reiki Certificates she was awarded at the end of her training to the trinkets that decorated the walk to the casket, and to the people who just needed to thank me for the teachings that were provided to her. Nothing would prepare me for what I would experience next.

Placed gently in her hands was the symbol of the chalice, a gift that I had given her at some juncture in her spiritual teachings. I held back every tear just so I could breathe. I immediately time traveled back to 1993 and remembered how the chalice was given to me. It was placed in my hands by the sacredness of love, as it was in hers. With every breath that I took at that moment, I realized that Sue would take with her the power and the love of what the symbol represents, as well as the power we hold to help someone else with their life journey. I understood that the vision I had fifteen years ago now had come full circle. Tears flooded my soul once more. I was immobilized with such sadness, until, in a distant sound, I heard Sue say, "Just help my family. I'm alright."

Through their tears, Sue's family told me that studying Reiki had changed her life. She was looking forward to helping people on their path to personal and spiritual growth and couldn't wait to pass along the gifts she had learned from this ancient art. I remembered how excited she was to participate in class, always enthusiastically asking and answering questions, and ready to help any one at any time. She was the embodiment of the reason why people love to teach.

My heart grieved with them as I felt her loss, made even more poignant by my friendship with her. I realized then how much influence we all have on each other's lives and how much our friendship matters to those we care about. It was humbling and powerful at the same time and I felt truly blessed to have been loved by this remarkable woman. I think a lot of us go through our lives unaware of the effect we have on our family and friends. For whatever reason, many of us find it hard to believe that each of us has the power to change someone's life. It can be through something as simple as a smile, a helping hand or a kind word. Or something as ultimately life changing as love.

I was reminded that Sue had been a force of love during her life, touching all those she met with openhearted sincerity and boundless joy. Her family told me how much my teachings had influenced her during her life and thanked me for giving her the gift of personal fulfillment. I told them how grateful I was to have known her.

In the next few days I prepared to meet with Sue's family at her residence. I went into deep prayer and meditation hoping that Sue would send some recognizable sign that would alleviate, even if for a brief millisecond of time, her grieving mother's heart and all the despair her whole family felt. I waited to hear a story to tell, but nothing would be shown to me until I sat at her kitchen table. Then it began. "Hello, I'm your father," I hear a gentleman say to Sue. "I've been waiting for you. I'm your father and I'm so glad to see you. I love you, my little girl."

Sue's father had died when she was two years old and she had never gotten to know him. I knew that Sue was overjoyed to make that connection just as her family was upon hearing this news. "She is good," I told them as I felt her energy join that of her father's. "She is doing all right. She is loving you from the other side. She is thanking you for loving her." I have to admit that

I was as happy as they were to hear this message.

Then came July 20, 2007. In one moment everything changed. Tullia, my dear friend, teacher, mentor, spiritual mother and companion, lay quietly in her bed on that last day. She was comfortable and incredibly peaceful as she bid farewell to those she loved. But it was not her voice that spoke to us. It was her spirit.

Her closest of friends were there, gathered together to give her strength and comfort. We stroked her with reassuring hands, gently loving and consoling her. But truth be told, it was us who needed the support. The memory of those final moments is forever branded within my soul and upon my mind. We sat beside her bed and waited for her to begin her journey home. Then, in an instant, she was gone.

In my work I have come to know grief and sorrow through the eyes of the thousands of people that I have met. Now I was forced to see it through my own eyes. I have seen so many of you at your most vulnerable points. Now I must acknowledge my own vulnerability. I've sat with you and prayed for you. I've always had deep compassion and sympathy for your loss. Now

I come to my own place of understanding what losing someone really means.

Though I am no expert in the field of loss, I speak directly from my heart to yours. To lose someone is not measured by anything anymore. It doesn't matter the person's age, their health, how they pass, how long it takes, what time it was or even knowing the bigger picture of such things. When you experience the death of a loved one in person, the hands of the clock barely seem to move.

As I sat with Tullia on that unforgettable July day, I waited for time to venture forward. I wondered why it took so long to get from one minute to the next. I realize now that those precious moments are what sustains me. It is in those moments that I can remember her smile, laughter and wisdom. Through her passing, I discovered that loss is a physical experience bouncing between the real events of life to the unreality of loss. You walk through moments helpless and hopeless. I've noticed that life is different than it was back in July of 2007, which now feels like centuries ago. The journey even feels awkward at times as you try to walk, breathe, live, and just be. Then in the next moment, it's all real again and life moves on.

The weeks after Tullia's death passed in

a blur of activity. Summer came and went, and before I knew it, the leaves started dressing in the colors of autumn.

My dear friend Cat had been ill for a long time, so her death was not as unexpected as the others. Cancer had created a tomb of her body. Her passing on October 19 was a mixed blessing, for as much as I was going to miss her dear friendship, I was relieved that she would now be pain free. She had been in a nursing home for several months and I made it a point to visit her as often as I could. We had said our goodbyes slowly during our last few visits, her eyes intimately revealing what was in her heart, my words showering her with love and support.

The day before she died, I had given a presentation in Chappaqua, New York. It was powerful as they always are and I met many wonderful people who were also grieving over the loss of those they loved. I ended the day feeling drained, both from the emotion that permeated the presentation and also because I was thinking about Cat. I woke from a restless sleep in the middle of the night knowing that I needed to visit Linda, one of the women I had met at the presentation, at her shop in Katonah, New York. The feeling to visit her overwhelmed me to the point of sleeplessness. Sometimes when a message is coming from spirit there is a persistent force behind it until the message is delivered completely and unconditionally. That is how it was this night until I heard what was needed to be heard. Finally after much prayer, the angels gently guided me back to slumber, nourishing my saddened heart with boundless love.

Shortly after getting out of bed the next morning, I received a call that Cat had quietly passed away in the arms of her best friend and family. After receiving the call, I was so grateful that I had taken the time to go home two days before to bid my friend goodbye and wish her well on her newfound journey to the beyond. It was evident that she knew it was me by the single tear that escaped from underneath her eyelash as I kissed her goodbye.

I had prayed about Cat all day long, and waited moment to moment with great anticipation for divine intervention. When I received the bad news, I intuitively knew that I needed to drive to Katonah, NY. The angels who had held my heavy heart the night before were pushing me to see Linda, in part because I had received another message from her friend, Ariel, who passed unexpectedly in a car accident in Florida a few weeks earlier, and in part because I too would receive healing from delivering the message.

Although she hadn't expected me, Linda was glad to see me and warmly welcomed me inside. I told her why I had come and gave her the message I was directed to deliver. As I did, I told her about Cat's passing. We both started to cry and hugged each other for support. That's when she asked if I would like to hear her friend Ariel's favorite song, "Somewhere Over the Rainbow," by the Hawaiian singer Iz. My heart skipped a beat. Wouldn't you know it, but that was one of Cat's favorite songs too. Signs from heaven have a way of comforting us when we need it most, and this was truly divinely inspired. I was grateful to take the CD with me for the car ride and left our visit with a lighter heart.

HEAVENLY SIGNS COMFORT US WHEN WE NEED IT MOST

I thought the song was the message I requested from spirit to guide me through my grief, but what came next was so precious and so precise that I know it was sent from God himself. It reminds me of the power that is within each of us. As we integrate the spiritual changes we receive, we create a connection that is unbreakable. With every ounce of faith and belief that we master, we receive a never-ending supply of spiritual blessings.

I was sitting in my car getting ready to go, "Somewhere Over the Rainbow" blaring as loud as could be, tears streaming down my red swollen face and sadness so deep that I could barely breathe. And then there was heaven...a license plate on the car in front of me that announced CAT 19. I looked up at the sky to say thank you for this heaven sent message and saw that it was filled with pink billowy clouds, like the ones Cat was so fond of painting. Coincidences? I think not. The synchronicities of life transcend time to offer us reassurance that love continues and that our prayers will be answered if only we have the courage to ask.

How have I changed through these experiences? I believe more firmly than ever that love does not die with the physical body. It is eternal. Our loved ones are but a moment away at all times. But even knowing this does not diminish the loss you feel after they pass. Sometimes even the quietness is haunting as you wait for the signs and sacred messages that life continues.

The last weeks of summer passed without a word from Tullia. It became disheartening for me to channel messages for my clients and not receive any myself. My grief spilled over to my daily life even as I tried to continue with my routine. But like each of you who have experienced such a loss, I learned that grief is a process and that there are certain things you can do to get through the pain.

Stand as tall as you can even when your body resists. Remember that loss is a physical experience, as it is emotional. Your body will ache. Your spirit will ache. Be kind to yourself. Rest as much as you can. Remember your inner strength. It's there and always has been there. Rely on yourself and your inner connection to faith. Call out for help, let someone in, and seek guidance if your sadness overwhelms you. If you need to scream out, scream out with a friend. Cry on someone's shoulders. Let them know how sad you really are. You don't have to battle this alone. Don't hold it in. Cry and cry, and cry some more. If someone wants to hold or hug you, let it happen. You are worthy to receive such a loving invitation.

BE KIND TO YOURSELF

Finally, do what you can to remember the joy, remember the memories and always remember the love. For this will make your heart smile.

I stepped back for a time while I privately grieved for my teacher, not wanting to face another day without her voice, touch and earthly support. It wasn't easy, but I somehow found my voice again. I began to speak of the bond Tullia and I shared and the knowing that heaven is all around us. Tullia remained silent for some six weeks before I heard from her again.

"It is time to move forward, Roland."

I heard Tullia whisper in my heart.

"It is time to continue your journey and tell people what you know to be true."

For all the years that I had known her, Tullia spent every August on a silent sabbatical. It was her time to pull back and reflect on her life, her beliefs and the teachings she shared with us all. She always told me that if we were silent, then all our dreams would be realized. She said that living with spirit required focus, concentration, dedication, commitment and perseverance and that we could manifest the greatest reality by being true to who we are. She practiced what she preached for one month a year, keeping her friends in her heart and thoughts but limiting any contact. In my pain over her passing, I had forgotten all about this time that we spent apart each year until it dawned on me that this is what

Tullia did every August.

When I finally would hear from her after her month of quiet solitude, she would share the thoughts and adventures she had experienced. She was always eager to impart the wisdom she had found in the stillness and silence. Could I expect the same this year?

NOURISH YOUR SOUL. SIT IN SILENCE. PRAY, MEDITATE AND LEARN

In the years before her passing, Tullia and I would spend countless hours discussing heaven. We would tell stories about the messages we received, visions we had encountered and experiences that further affirmed the existence of eternal love. As unbelievable as it sounds, there were many times when we witnessed the same spiritual communications, both of us being touched by heavenly beings and messages at the same time. She was especially supportive of this book, believing that it would be an important source of healing for all of us on our journey of love. She spoke of it often during those last months, when she turned to me as my spiritual teacher and mentor and said that I needed to tell the whole story with love and compassion for the benefit of humanity. She told me she would always be there to guide my hand, to help illuminate the messages that so many people needed to hear. "All is in Divine Order," she would say over and over again in times of difficulty. I found it hard to accept that in the moments right after she was gone, until I recalled more of what she taught me.

"Death is the wisdom to perceive beyond illusion. You will know that living and dying is merely a frame in a motion picture, a light playing on the wall. Death is a doorway that does not close. And you may know, now and forever, that I will never leave you no matter where I go." Her words carried her truth in life and in death as I was about to find out with more certainty than ever in the weeks that followed.

ELEVEN

BEYOND THE VEIL

MEMORIES THAT HAD BEEN too painful for me to revisit came flooding back and I was transported to Tullia's apartment, a sanctuary where we spent many cherished moments together, now empty of her physical presence. Once a place filled with glorious antiquities and photographs of a life well lived was at this moment sketched with faded memories that seemed to slip further away with every passing moment. The oil paintings and sacred artifacts that had graced the walls of her home lay in silent refuge. In some distant place I hear my beloved Tullia's voice and I know that soon she will tell her story. But for the moment, I need only wait and believe.

Tullia's sister had traveled from Switzerland with a friend to attend to Tullia's personal affairs, later gathering with us in Tullia's apartment to help pack up her most cherished belongings for shipment abroad. We all grieved at the loss of our dear friend and sister and silently hoped for a message to comfort our aching hearts.

In the blink of an eye, the room was smothered with love and filled with angelic authority. An entourage of mystical beings escorted Tullia here along with a younger man I had never met. He must speak first I hear. So I listen. His mother had traveled a long distance to act as an interpreter for Tullia's sister, who spoke only French. I say to her with serenity in my voice "your boy...your boy can still smile at you." After catching her breath, smoking a cigarette to calm her nerves and coming to terms with our conversation, she tells me that the only memory that is left in her mind is her son's smile, everything else is gone.

MEMORIES ARE SOUL MARKINGS REMINDING US OF A LIFE OF LOVE

The love, the angels, the spiritual radiance seem to be everywhere now and it was everything I needed. My hair stands from one end of my body to the other and a gentleness fills my heart with such unexplainable joy. I am so pleased to see that Tullia has made her way back to me, to all of us. What I see with my eyes is the presence of a woman whom I love eternally. I see her weightless, body, mind and spirit. The light that surrounded her for as long as I have known her is still hers. Her smile is healing, her touch is heavenly and her words the same...that there is not death as we know it.

She communicated with me telepathically, her voice resonating within my heart. She begins to tell me where she has been and each word must be carefully translated for her sister into French so the essence of this story is understood. Tullia speaks of the journey that she has embarked on from her last breath in the physical world to her pilgrimage to spirit. It was more beautiful and more Godly than any moment of her entire existence. Again she communicates with such gratitude to all of us for the love she received in the days prior to her departure to the next place. She whispers so gently in my ear that she was happy to go home, to finally have the freedom from the suffering, and to be totally free from the painful captivity of a deteriorating body. She was able to leave us without hesitation because she knew it was right. She understood that suffering in itself was a teacher for her as it may be for all of us, to learn patience and trust, to acknowledge faith and devotion, and not to give up. If you give up, then you have misplaced God, divinity and all the light that is within you.

She stood at heaven's doorway with her

soul stretching beyond the veil, like that of a child waiting for the treasures and

THE LAST BREATH IS FILLED WITH GOD

trinkets of life. Tullia saw the staircase, walked, then ran to it knowing that it meant freedom and flight for her. She was escorted by her assigned souls; guides, masters and teachers that she loved so dearly. She told me that these guides and spirits are transparent, and luminescent and made only of love. I am reminded of what I have learned in my spiritual life thus far, that each of us will be escorted to the healing sanctuary, a place of extraordinary renewal as we take our last breaths. The last breath is a brief milli-moment of life changing aloneness that is filled with God, and God alone. This is when you enter the realm of total and utter compassion and unconditional love fills you beyond your wildest imagination.

She spoke of how her last breath was the greatest gift she ever experienced. She told me as the month of August passed by all of us that her silence was inevitable and necessary for her own evolution into the realities of the beyond. We are to be tireless proponents of looking within, as she taught us by being a living example of what finding spirituality is within the stillness of silence.

A life without her voice would challenge me, as it does you with those that you miss. Somehow the voice reshapes itself as it fades into other sacred entities on our journeys, divine messages of hope delivered by a friend, a butterfly sitting quietly upon a window sill, a hummingbird stopped in front of you as you gaze into the sunset and songs that appear in the most synchronized moments of life.

THE VOICE RESHAPES ITSELF AS IT FADES INTO OTHER SACRED ENTITIES

She sat in quiet meditation awakening to the gift of the heart. I could see her and then all of us at the temple of healing, and in that instant I was attuned to a greater frequency of understanding. In that brief moment I understood with such clarity that I too will be awakened to that essence of myself when the time is right.

Why wait? I must tell you that today is that day for all of us to be peaceful, harmonious and compassionate as we live our lives to the fullest knowing that these are ingredients for a blessed life. We can heighten our awareness and consciousness, we can heal, and we can love, and we can begin this life-altering process before the end of this journey.

Tullia went to a place she called home. Heaven's wings reached out for her and guided her to be the sacred sage that we all knew she was. She was greeted by her teachers, by her friends and then by her mother. I described to her during one of my many hospital visits, heaven's splendor and beauty, when her voice was silenced by the mechanics of survival. She said my understanding of what heaven was, was exactly what she had witnessed. I told her that heaven is a place where our free will is not depleted by the loss of the body, and our heart is tuned to its true sound. I spoke of how heaven holds our hands as we release the encased sadness to breathtaking awesomeness that grows moment by moment, never ending.

WE CAN SEE THE HEAVENLY ARMS REACHING FOR US

I know that there is a brief, ever so brief moment after our last physical breath that we begin to move into our true selves. This moment is more precious than any gem of life. It is a moment when we see all that we have ever known and bear witness to it in ways we've never done before. Here, on the journey to the heavenly dwelling, you lose your fear to be who you really are. In that crystal clear moment we are realigned with the divine love that exists within us and it is a moment to be cherished. Beyond the veil we can see the arms of heaven reaching for us. Then the angels, heavenly souls, teachers, masters and our ancestors all guide us to the book of our life on a journey beyond anything we can possibly imagine. It is a reward for a life well lived, for earthly moments defined by unconditional love, compassion and service to others. It is the culmination of a lifetime of learning, of mastering life's lessons and reaching the best part of you. It's what life, love, God, spirit and faith are all about.

I was offered a rare glimpse of that moment when I made my way up the heavenly staircase so many years ago. Words cannot do justice to what I experienced there. I remember trying to describe what I saw and felt to my closest friends, hoping to share with them the exultation that permeated every part of my being. That proved to be a most daunting task, because no matter how hard I tried to convey the divine essence of that heavenly journey, I somehow fell short of an adequate description. It was so much more than I could ever verbally express.

Tullia and I used to spend hours upon hours talking about our visions of heaven, how to become an enlightened person and how to live life fully, both of us sharing our most intimate views and divinely inspired experiences. As spiritual soul mates, we felt a unique kinship that transcended the physical world. We saw spirits at the same time, heard the messages and felt their energy in such synchronicity that it confirmed life beyond physical death. I believe in the power of the moment, the sanctity of faith and the promise of hope. If we fulfill all the aspects that I believe define a well-lived life—love unconditionally, live fully in union with humanity, extend compassion to all, and respect each other—then the promise of heaven, beyond, above and within, a gift like no other is yours.

We talked often and long, discussing the existence of the life force, and the eternal energy it brings. She used to recite sacred texts and especially loved "there has never been a time when you or I did not exist. And there will never be a time when we cease to exist. Physical bodies appear and disappear, but the atma, the soul, the life force lives on." This teaching illuminates the essence of the true self, that it is continuous and ever evolving. Imagine for a moment that you breathe into a cup. If the cup falls apart, the air is still present. Your essence, your oneness is not gone. The cup reminds us that the physical body will cease to exist, but the life force, the soul, the essence continues to survive beyond the illusion of the cup.

Tullia was an avid believer in looking within for answers and finding spirituality in the stillness of silence. When she passed away on July 20, 2007, I wondered when and if our conversations would continue. I must tell you that I was not looking forward to a world without her voice. I dreaded the silence caused by her absence even though she herself would remind me of the necessity and benefit of the still mind. She understood that stillness was a vital life force, and as we breathed it in, it freed us from the restlessness and the unsettledness of the moment. I knew that when I was in my solitude, she and my spiritual entourage would sit quietly by my side, reaching for me with tenderness and understanding. But I longed for Tullia to break the quiet and resume our cherished conversations.

In reality I didn't have to wait too long even though at the time it seemed forever. She came to me a few months after she passed, eager to share with me what she had been doing since she left. She talked about the healing she received on the stairway to heaven, shedding all the sorrows she had closely guarded in her heart during her life. I realized with more certainty that we will be awarded the same opportunity if we choose it. She was guided, as we all will be when we are ready to move onward and upward, where teachings resume in earnest. She said she knew I would be all right after she left and that she was always within my reach. I wrote her words on a piece of paper as she spoke so that I could remember everything she imparted to me. We had agreed a long time ago that they be shared in this book. When the time came to include them, I couldn't find the paper on which they were written. There must be a reason I thought then, knowing that when the time was right I would find it again.

I was in a meeting at a friend's house when Tullia reminded me of what I had written on that lost piece of paper. My friend and I had gotten together to talk about this book and the stories which were to be included in this chapter. I knew this chapter in particular would be very emotional for me and I was glad for her support.

As I entered her dining room, I was overcome with an odd and overwhelming sensation of choking and I felt like my lungs were filling up with fluid. I coughed as I felt my chest tighten and looked around the room for the offending presence.

"Is that your father?" I asked my friend as I walked over to a photograph of a man sitting on the top shelf of her corner hutch. "He wants to speak to you but he always found it difficult to talk to you." My friend laughed, clearly knocked off guard by this unexpected event, but still acknowledging the truth of that statement. Oh boy, he's intense I thought as I looked at him. "He wants to tell you something right now. He has a lot to say."

My friend looked embarrassed and offered to remove the photo in the hope that I would feel more comfortable and we could talk as planned. "That wouldn't do any good," I explained. "Your father's energy is here and he isn't leaving until he says what he needs to say. Do I have permission to speak to you freely?" I asked my friend.

As I let his spirit speak, my choking began to abate and I started to breathe again. I told her that her father had felt that he had betrayed her as a child, choosing to ignore her for other pressing matters in his life. "He is sorry that he didn't take your hand when you were a little girl and was relieved when you stopped reaching for him. He said you were always a free spirit and he didn't 'get' you. He had to be serious and focused in life and secretly envied you for your lighthearted ways and happy-go-lucky outlook. He couldn't talk to you because of it."

Her father asked for his daughter's forgiveness and promised to help her on her path, offering the love and support he couldn't give during his lifetime. I could see her heart open and her spirit lighten as I talked, witnessing a healing long overdue and the blossoming of a relationship that never had the chance to grow on earth.

At the time, we both wondered what that was all about for she was as surprised as I was to hear a message from her father who had lost his battle with lung cancer more than 17 years ago, a man who stayed a stranger her entire life. We didn't have to wonder for long as Tullia made her way into my heart, answering the questions I had been asking for months after she left.

"I've been resting in the arms of my mother," she said. "I have been wrapped in her embrace since I left." She went on to tell me that she had been basking in her mother's love for 31 days after she passed away, 31 days of unconditional love that she had never known from her mother in life. She healed the heartache she had carried with her from childhood and was now complete. She was ready to move on with her teachers and masters who waited for her to join them in a place at the top of those brilliant white stairs.

It's funny how spirit gives us lessons with precision timing. Tullia's anguish concerning her mother was her first order of business on a healing step in heaven. My friend was given the opportunity to forgive her father and feel his love before taking the next step of her life's journey.

On the glistening stairway to our heavenly sanctuary we have a chance to go back, to right a wrong, to heal the wounds that distressed us in life, to give compassion to a moment that needed it and to bring love to moments that were without it. We see our *Book of Life* before us and are blessed with the infinite possibility of pausing on the pages that need to be read again.

I believe we remain in the healing energy until that part of our soul is complete once again. Then we move forward on the next step of our journey towards that heavenly palace that waits at the top of the stairs.

TWELVE

A GRATEFUL HEART

THANK YOU. The power of these two small words knows no bounds. They have the miraculous ability to brighten someone's day, to lighten a heavy heart and to make someone smile. They can open new doors, forge friendships, restore confidence and attract abundance, both here on earth and in heaven.

These words continue to change my life every day, as I know they do for so many of my clients. I have seen them transform grief into hope in private sessions and group presentations, as loved ones who have passed extend their gratitude from the heavens beyond. I have witnessed them turn doubt into belief and I have seen them melt hearts hardened by years of misunderstanding. In fact, some of the most rewarding aspects of my role as a channel are the "thank yous" I receive for passing along the messages.

"I just wanted to thank you for an amazing evening. Your message from my grandmother was just perfect. I called her "Ma" and she called me "Dawnie." The fact that you were able to convey

MESSAGES ARE TO BE HEARD IF WE LISTEN

this message from beyond, complete with names, was touching and proved to me that there are messages to be heard if we listen!" *Dawn*

"I just really wanted to thank you for your service work last night in Wilton. The messages you delivered were really helpful to me. When you got the message about how my mother died—that she had some sort of stroke that suddenly hit her and it went dark for her—I knew you were right on. I had worried about whether or not she saw it coming or felt any pain, but your message from her was clear. I didn't tell you that my mom had a freak car accident on the way to pick me up from the airport for Christmas and never made it. You mentioned that she was in a healing place right now and not communicating a lot, but what you were able to share meant so much to me. Thank you for the work you do." *Mary*

"Thank you, Roland, for helping me find peace and harmony in my life and for learning how to quietly listen for God's voice. I especially thank you for helping me come to terms with my father's passing and allowing him to come back into my life from the other side today...on what would have been his 80th birthday!" *Christine*

"When I last saw you, you told me that my deceased father would be sending me a red bird in one month. Well about a month later, I was moving the last of his belongings out of his condo, one of which was a beautiful stained glass cardinal he had hanging in his window. Thank you Roland." *Barbara*

"Thank you so much. I left your presentation feeling drained, yet at some kind of peace. I was hoping to bring some items of my sister who died in a boating accident in 1996 with me to the presentation but I left work late. I came home and was trying to locate a card I had written for her wedding shower. I couldn't find it, so I quickly grabbed a ring that was given to her by her old boyfriend. I was in a little panic that I lost the card and wondered where it could be. Since my sister died so young in her 30s, I

GRATITUDE HAS THE MIRACULOUS ABILITY TO BRIGHTEN SOMEONE'S DAY don't have many items of hers.

You mentioned the book in your presentation and said to find the book. I knew immediately what book it was. I had given her a book called *Sisters* one Christmas. It was found in her house on her night table and my mother gave it back to me when she passed.

I was a little surprised when you mentioned it. I had read it 11 years ago and could not find any message in it. But I came home and took it out anyway. Inside was the card I was looking for, a card she gave me, two pictures and a letter I had written for a trial about the accident. I was shocked to say the least.

Thank you so much. The most important message I heard was that it doesn't matter the reason or how she died. It was not a pretty death and it took them many hours to locate her and her husband's bodies. You told me that my sister said, 'Let it go. It doesn't matter.'

That has been one of the things I couldn't get past. The night replays in my mind now for 11 years. You also said she is beautiful (which was so important to her) and that she is in heaven. I have felt her around me for years. It was so nice to be in a room full of people that get that. What a beautiful evening." *Debbie*

"I met with you in August to hear messages from my daughter Meagan who died in a car crash. I played for you the message she left on her cell phone a week after she passed away. You assured me that the message was from her and that other messages would follow. You were absolutely right and I have received numerous signs and messages from her, usually when I am at my lowest point. My visit with you brought me such comfort and hope, such assurance that my precious daughter lives on. I thank you so much for sharing yourself with us and looking forward to meeting with you again." *Carolyn*

"I know you are busy, but I need to take a minute to thank you for what you have given me. The messages that you have given me about my grandfather and cousin are so precious, I cannot even begin to explain. Seeing and hearing how my grandfather came to me through you... his personality, things I said to him, etc. changed my life. They were so healing. Thank you for sharing your amazing gift with me." *Christy*

In my line of work, thank yous come from the heavens too. Many of the messages I receive from spirit are to share their appreciation and gratitude for what their loved ones did for them when they were together.

"Dean," I say to an older man in one of my presentations. "There is a woman standing next to your right shoulder. She wants to thank you for everything you did for her. She said there wasn't anything left to do; you couldn't fix her. You did everything you could. She said you made her feel like a queen and she knows you miss her. She never wanted for anything. Thank you, she says, thank you for loving her as much as you did." She wasn't through just yet. "Thank you for coming here tonight even though this isn't your kind of thing. I love you." I realized at that moment that she had also given me a message in the morning that I had written down in my pad. I retrieved it from the front of the room and gave it to him, folded. There in writing was another thank you for sharing his life with her.

"There is a boy here who committed suicide," I announce in a group session. He has a message for his mother. A woman named Ellen acknowledges the loss of her son and I tell her that he has been waiting to talk to her.

"He's here with you and he's not struggling anymore. He wants to thank you for your love and support. He is not crying anymore," he says.

"He says he didn't tell you the whole story in his note but it's all straightened out now. He is grateful that you always listened to the stories he wrote since he was six years old. He is going to be a messenger now and will send you a story from the other side. 'Thank you for believing in me Mom,' he says.

OUR BELOVED PETS ENTER THE HEAVENLY KINGDOM

"Jake the dog. Joy. Going home. Thank you for taking such good care of me" reads one of the notes I had written the morning before a presentation. No one claimed it, until a week later when I spoke to a woman who had put her ailing 15-year old lab to sleep the day I wrote the message. "He can walk again," I tell her over the phone, hearing the relief and gratitude in her voice.

Many of my clients ask if their loved ones can still see and hear them from the other side. Of course they can I tell them. Every time you ask, they are there. They can hear every word you want them to hear, share in your accomplishments and see those who are important to you in this life. Rest assured, they're only with you when you need them to be.

"Karen," I call out to a woman who has come to my Celebration of Angels presentation.

This presentation is designed to be a workshop to help people connect with their angels, rather than a channeled message session, but after reading this book, I think you know how it goes. It seems that whenever and wherever I meet with people who want to make a spiritual connection, the messages flow with a greater intensity and purpose.

"Your father's here," I tell her. He says, "That's my girl." He is so proud of you, you know. He's all dressed up and says that he has a lot going on."

Karen smiles and is not at all surprised that he has remained a corporate executive-type on the other side.

"He wants you to know that he wasn't an expert on this place before he left. He says he didn't believe in it."

She nods in agreement, remembering their long talks about the absence of any scientific proof about heaven and the possibility of an after-life.

"He's an expert now he says and he knows all about heaven now." You know, he didn't believe in heaven, or God, or angels or spirits when he was here. He does now. He wants to thank you for helping your mother. "He wasn't easy with her," he says. He wants you to know how much he loves you and that he is always with you. Keep talking to him, he says; he still enjoys your conversations and he hears every word. "Thank you for being my girl," he says.

Given his lifelong philosophical analysis and subsequent skepticism about the existence of God and heaven, his words were especially powerful to her. They were also just what she longed to hear. She wiped away her tears and thanked me for validating what she knew to be true in her heart.

Not everyone I meet is as accepting of the messages as the people you have read about here. I do a monthly radio show at a local station in Connecticut where I am available to give messages to callers who phone in. Due to time limitations, the messages are short, but personal, perhaps seeming a little too vague to the average listener, but uniquely meaningful to the caller. The host of the show is unfailingly amazed at how the phone lines light up during my hour with him and is always supportive of the messages that are conveyed on the air. I look forward to these appearances as much as he and his listeners do and make sure I leave ample time to prepare for his show.

One winter day, the weather was stormy with ice-driven sleet and snow and the driving was treacherous. I arrived at the station early to be sure that I would not disappoint the show's listeners. The regular host, however, was not so fortunate and the bad road conditions prevented him from making it to the show on time. So his associate filled in for him and, as luck would have it, he was either in ill humor, visibly frazzled about the extra workload he had to assume because of the weather, or he was a determined non-believer in anything that could not be factually explained. I was not prepared for his on-air confrontation.

His introduction caught me off guard and was more of a challenge than anything else. He was reading promotional copy that his staff had prepared for him.

"It says here that you are a channel who conveys messages from people who have died," he began. Before I could acknowledge his words, he said, "Well, that's a lot of bunk that just prays on the vulnerability of people who have lost loved ones. It's a scam."

His taunts continued and I felt myself becoming defensive as he deliberately provoked me and pushed my buttons. I felt my face turn red, as he challenged me to contact his deceased mother and give him a message. He was intense in his insistence and quite obviously skeptical of what I did.

"I don't have a message from your mother," I said somewhat defiantly just as we went off the air for a commercial break. I took a few very deep breaths and looked around the station hoping that our conversation would end. Before I knew it, I felt the presence of a spirit who was making her way to me. It was his mother and she was giving me an earful.

"Your mother is here," I told him and "she wants you to know that she is glad we have met. She speaks of her last days and of your persistence in taking care of her. She knows what you did for her. She wants me to give you a note."

His face paled and he looked at me with a quizzical expression as I began writing down a message from his mother. I handed it to him at the same time as the regular host arrived and quickly took over the broadcast. Our altercation was over, but my experience with this radio personality was not finished.

He explained that his mother had passed away a year earlier. He put a note in her casket telling her how much he loved her just before her casket was closed for the last time. The note I gave him was a heartfelt answer to his prayers. It simply said, "I love you too."

As honored as I feel after moments like these, I have to remind everyone that their gratitude should be directed to their loved ones, not at me. For they are the ones who will always watch over and love them just as they did when they were together. That's one of the reasons that I used to leave journals out in my office so that my clients could write personal messages. I know they mean as much to those in spirit as they do to those who write them. They are true gifts of the heart.

"Dear Gram, It's been almost 21 years since you left me and our family. I miss you still so much. Thanks for coming to me through Roland and telling me how much you love me and that you're proud of me. I am taking care of Papa as much as I can. I know you two have been apart for a long time and I know he misses you too. Thanks for watching over me, protecting me and sending me guidance. I still need you in my life. You are always and will always be in my heart. I love you. Thanks for all you do for me." Love, *Donna*

A SIMPLE THANK YOU CAN CHANGE THE WORLD

"Dear Dad and Grandma, I am so glad you both were with me tonight and for helping me from the other side. Please continue to give me the strength I need to take care of my mom. Thank you for coming to Roland and giving me the peace of mind that I so need." Love always, *Suzanne*

"Bob, I knew you would come! I know you loved me, you said it enough. I will look for the nickels. We now have closure. I know now that you are at peace. You are missed so very much." Love, *Eloise*

"Thank you Dad and Nan. I always knew you were watching over me. It was so relieving to know that you are really here and listening to me. I'm glad you know about Adriana and I am so happy that you are happy and pain free. Please stay close by. I need your strength and love to sustain me." *Lori*

"Dearest Kerry, thank you so very much for answering me. You know how much you have helped me, you can see it and I so much appreciate it. Miss you terribly. Please take care of my mom," Love you always, *Jackie*

These thank you notes are written from the purest of places and sent from hearts bursting with love. Do not doubt for a minute the power they have to heal both here and in heaven. For the moment these feelings of gratitude are acknowledged, they are delivered to the ones who are waiting to hear them.

A simple thank you. It has the power to make a difference on heaven and earth.

THIRTEEN

A CELEBRATION OF ANGELS

I HAVE BEEN CHANNELING messages professionally for more than twenty-five years. My work has taken me down the street, across state lines and around the world. My clients are male and female, black and white and yellow, straight and gay, young and old, rich and poor, healthy and infirm. I've met with people from all walks of life, married, single, widowed, divorced, with children and without. I've done readings for those who were just starting out and those who were on top of their game. I've helped people cross over and consoled loved ones left behind. I've counseled lost souls who were down on their luck and others whose lives seemed charmed. I've seen them in groups and by themselves, at private homes and public venues. I have talked with them on air during radio broadcasts, on TV programs and through Internet pod casts. And as diverse as my clients are, they all share a desire to make an angelic spiritual connection that affirms that through the imperfection of life the perfect is always present.

Once you have a moment like the many I have had in my life you become **YOUR** very aware that the possibility of spiritual communication exists **HEART** in this present reality. The inner **HEARS IT,** power, the confidence and the ability to hold the quietness affords **SEES IT** you many opportunities to expand **AND FEELS** your connection to those you love and miss, and to the universal **IT FIRST** splendor that is above, beyond and within. Truthfully speaking, you have to learn how to relate differently, to become a beacon of understanding that it's not your voice that guides the communication now but your heart. Your heart hears it first, feels it first and somehow knows it first. Somewhere between the knowing in your heart and the explanation in your head, doubts can creep in. That is where someone like me comes in. Not to announce your message or to do it for you or even to tell you what to do, but to support you, to validate you and to share that the messages that have been sent to you are divinely guided in the here and now. I am here to tell you that what you feel in your heart is real.

Have you ever felt a rush of warmth when you thought about a loved one who has passed or smelled the scent of a favorite flower or perfume they may have loved? Maybe you saw a robin in a January snowstorm or a rainbow in the middle of nowhere under the noonday sun. You might have woken up from a dream encounter that was so vivid and detailed that you could have sworn it was real. Or heard the distinctive chime of a bell in a quiet room. You could have a sudden onset of goose bumps, chills moving up and down your spine, a tingling in your fingers and toes or be moved to tears or laughter for no apparent reason. This is how spiritual signs manifest. This is how you can tell when the angels and your loved ones are trying to get your attention. This is what you might experience when they are sending a message to you. These are affirmations that they are still here.

THE MESSAGE RECEIVED IS THE MESSAGE NEEDED

There are a lot of other signs as well. They could be coins like the 16 cents that inspired me and thousands of others to have faith on their journey, the feather that I found on my pillow after I prayed about a little girl who was murdered in an unsolved cold case to show me a sign that it was truly her that I felt in my presence and the picture I drew of Archangel Michael at his request, on March 21, 2001, at 9:25 PM with five minutes to spare before my 9:30 PM telephone session with a woman from Kentucky. The 16 cents are safely ensconced in a frame. The feather is protected in a plastic sleeve to remind me that the all too brief life of a little girl will not be forgotten and the picture of the most glorious angel of all hangs on my office wall as a reminder that spirit is in everything and is all around us.

One of the most amazing things is that we perceive the message as we need to hear it or see it, exactly as it is intended to be. To realize that a message is there is the first step on this amazing spiritual journey. Take for instance, the magic of that painting I created in 5 minutes. Long strands of color that spread over the paper like peacock feathers in blue and purple, a heart in the center etched with silver metallic and glitter light, and the images of tiny splatters of paint that illuminate the possibility of angelic forces. To me it was just a painting filled with divine energy until the following day when I just happened to open a book on angels. On one of the pages it clearly stated that "Archangel Michael has colors of blue and purple to show his protection and solidarity to the heavens often in reference to peacock feathers." To me this moment was a gift, for that is exactly how I painted Archangel Michael.

This is the second step; acknowledging that the message is a gift. My painting hangs in my office for all to see and often I take it with me, but nothing ever so beautiful as my mother insisting that this painting looked just like a vase. Life is all a matter of perception, a walk beyond the illusion into what you know as your truth.

I am blessed to still have these items in my possession to remind me what my journey is all about. I am also grateful to be able to help others see the signs that were directed to them.

I remember one very emotional session I had years ago with a woman whose best friend was murdered. As she walked in the office I was working from, I heard five gunshots as distinctly as if they were being shot right at that moment in my office. I closed my eyes and the vision of her friend's murder played out like a movie with unmistakable clarity. Her wounds and the stillness that followed were crystal clear to me. Then to my amazement, rainbows danced inside my mind, dozens of them, filling the sky above her. I knew that her friend was carried safely to heaven by a legion of beautiful angels.

"I have a message for you from your friend," I said to my client. "She says she has a job in heaven. She paints rainbows." As I described the scene of her murder, she confirmed its accuracy with inconsolable tears. And I knew in that moment heaven spoke once more.

The woman understood her message immediately. For it seemed that she had already been finding rainbows when she least expected them and she had seen them just about everyday since her friend had passed.

Signs. They are everywhere if you only open your heart to them. One thing that I truly understand is the persistence of the angelic messenger. A constant unbreakable series of events that synchronistically realign your life until the meaning of that message is understood. I also have come to understand that if we choose to learn and grow in each moment of our lives, the angelic spiritual team will shower you with loving support until the time is right to embrace the Godly message. The spiritual world is patient.

Nancy's friend Bob was determined to get a message to her. He would not take no for an answer during my presentation on Gratitude because he wanted to respond to her prayers that she would see him again. Well, it turns out that since he had passed a few years before, he had tried several times to get her attention.

Nancy's daughters threw her a wonderful 80th birthday celebration with all her friends and family. Before their guests arrived, Nancy went into her bathroom to adjust her hair and make-up. As she looked in the bathroom mirror, she saw the initials RWO on her mirror, clear as day. They were written in soap.

Now during their courtship, Bob used to leave Nancy messages on her mirror, messages he always wrote using a bar of soap. He often put a heart sticker on the mirror, too, to remind her how much he loved her.

Nancy showed both her daughters and Bob's son the message on the mirror. His son confirmed that it was indeed his father's handwriting and one of the unique ways he left reminders around the house when he was alive.

The following summer, Nancy was awakened with a loud thud at the foot of her bed. She spoke of this with a lighter heart, saying that it happened right after she asked Bob to give her a sign that he was listening to her.

Still she asked for more messages, fearful that she might have only imagined what she so desired. Bob's insistent presence during my Gratitude presentation came through loud and clear and Nancy finally came to believe that the signs and messages were real.

Nancy is not alone in her hesitancy to accept signs. Many people dismiss them as figments of their imagination. Anthony was afraid to believe in signs as well until one day the sign was too real to explain away.

He came to me for many sessions to help him get through the loss of his father and later a break-up with the woman he had been dating. A no-nonsense kind of guy, Anthony owned a fitness center and was prone to dealing in the physical rather than in the spiritual realm.

One day during a particularly intense workout, he watched in disbelief as a pigeon walked in through his front door. It was a beautiful day, with warm sunshine and a fresh breeze that filled the studio with the promises of spring. Anthony had propped the door open to take advantage of the great weather, but of course, he never expected a bird to walk in and make himself at home. The pigeon circled around the fitness equipment, taking his time to look around. Then, quite unexpectedly, he slammed his body into the full-length mirror that lined the wall of the studio and subsequently fell to the floor. Stunned but unhurt, he picked himself up and walked right out the door.

Anthony continued his cardio training, amused at what had just taken place. After he finished his training, he went to clean the smudge left on the mirror by the pigeon. He also picked up a stray feather left behind by the wandering bird and threw it out the front door.

But that's not the end of the story. The next day a photographer who was working out with Anthony inquired about the smudge on the mirror. Anthony was surprised that his client could see it, for he had cleaned it off the night before. Blessed with a detailed eye, the photographer remarked that the smudge looked just like a man's face, with each defining feature clearly laid out before him. So intrigued was he that he took out his camera and photographed it. What he and Anthony, and all the others who have viewed it since, saw in that photo was a clear likeness of Anthony's deceased father, along with the image of Anthony's dog who had also recently passed.

YOU MUST BELIEVE IT BEFORE YOU CAN SEE IT

What's more, the feather that Anthony had thrown out had reappeared by the mirror, below the smudge that couldn't be cleaned away. Anthony has fastened the feather and framed photograph on a wall near the smudge, which is now fading with time. But the connections that tie Anthony together with his father and dog have only strengthened after this experience.

The power of believing before seeing is the greatest navigational system given to man. This power guides you and opens you to a place beyond yourself. It expands your consciousness and awareness to a new level of understanding. It gives you the strength to believe that initials could be etched upon a mirror and, and a feather strangely makes it way back to where it started from. By no means are these mistakes. These are divine interventions to get us to be thoughtful, and reflective of the power of love and faith. If we doubt the message then we doubt the possibility of continued love from those that have left us.

Sara lost her husband Michael six months after their wedding. They were involved in a hit and run car crash in which she lived and he passed away. She was pregnant when he died, carrying both the burden of grief and the miracle of life by herself in the difficult days that followed. Six months to the day of the accident, she prayed for a sign from him. She got so much more than she had ever dared hope for.

I met Sara at a presentation in Stamford. I also met Michael at that presentation, a vibrant young spirit who was eager to share what was in his heart. He told me about the accident, how he left immediately, how he watched as the fire engines valiantly doused the flames caused by the impact and how they tended to Sara with heroic compassion as they tried in vain to shield her from his own early demise. He showed me the crossroads where he and the other driver met in a tangle of steel, only to have the perpetrator speed off into the darkness leaving a wreckage of lives and love lost.

"I love you, I love you, I love you," he repeated over and over again with such a gentleness that it nearly brought me to tears. "I know about our baby and am watching over her from my chair," he said through me. "I am her guardian angel now and I will always be with her."

Sara told me that she had placed her husband's favorite chair in her daughter's room so that a part of him would always be there with the two of them. She acknowledged that her daughter would often point at the chair and smile at some unseen presence. Sara had known in her heart that Michael still sat in that chair.

I continued sharing his messages, telling her that Michael is still talking about the wedding, that he thought he looked great that day—yes he still had that same sense of humor that made her laugh when they were together in life—and that she was and always would be the love of his life. Then he gave Sara a message that she would never forget.

"I sent you a sign, just like you asked, Sara," said Michael. "I sent you Chris."

Sara had not come to my presentation alone. She had come with Chris. Chris had been a childhood friend of Michael's and was on hand to help Sara out after his friend's tragic death. After a wonderful friendship, they unexpectedly fell in love. It seems that Michael had orchestrated their relationship from above. He knew that Chris would take great care of Sara and the baby and he knew they would make a loving family. He was grateful that it was working out just as he had hoped.

Sara and Chris left the presentation early, their faces glistening first with tears of sorrow and of moments lost, then glowing with love, for Michael, for each other, and for the baby they now rushed home to.

I was privileged to travel to Ireland a few years back for a presentation with a group of people from the United States. Everything about that trip was amazing, from the magnificent castle hotel we stayed in to the royal dinner banquets fit for a king to the signs that manifested during this experience.

We had just finished our session for the evening when I was making my way down a turreted staircase to my room. I met a young couple on the stairs and was compelled to share the messages I had for them. With their permission I asked to share what I felt in that moment, they were not part of our group so my comments took them by complete surprise.

"Your grandmother thanks you for the yellow rose you left for her on the chair yesterday," I said to the young man whose instant response was jaw dropping, red faced, and tearful as sorrow clutched him from head to toe. I turned to his wife and said the exact same thing. She was unable to speak. She stood with her arms folded attempting to figure out the extent of that moment.

They both looked at me with quizzical looks, probably thinking that this complete stranger was more than a little crazy. But after explaining who I was and my mission of delivering words of comfort from beyond, it dawned on them what the messages meant. At their wedding the day before our chance meeting, each of them had put a yellow rose on empty chairs reserved for their grandmothers who had passed away years before the wedding. And while the messages were by themselves amazing, what was equally significant was the fact that this young couple lived under an hour away from me in the United States. Our meeting on the stairs of an ancient Irish castle was not by chance or coincidence. It was so I could impart the messages meant for them, present them with a gift from their grandmothers on one of the most important occasions of their lives, their honeymoon.

It seemed that every day of my trip to Ireland was more amazing than the last, not just for the people who waited anxiously for a message from their loved ones who had passed, but for those of us who witnessed the healing that took place whenever a connection was made. On the first day of our gathering, I took a question from a woman who was visibly distraught and quite anxious to hear what messages I had for her. She had spent a lifetime wondering about a man she had never met but whom she had hoped with all her heart to come to know. My answer was instantaneous. The words "You have come to hear about your biological father, stepfather and foster father" played like a symphony of sound in my mind and then joyfully continued with "your father wants me to tell you that when the butterfly lands and only when the butterfly lands will you know how much love there is for you." At that moment of my presentation there was complete silence, even from the wait staff. Everyone from every corner of this grand ballroom gazed upon this woman and began to feel her pain. In that moment we became one, as I see so many times at my events. A hand touches another, a smile stretches gently, and eyes gleam compassion, and the love in the room is palpable.

Ten days later on the last day of the last meal and the last chance for a prayer to be answered, a scream that bordered on insanity shook all ninety of us. The microphone sputtered a screeching sound. Then over the intercom system we heard "Roland Comtois, the butterfly has landed." There soaring in the room, with wings expanded elegantly, the most beautiful yellow butterfly was parading through the room like that of a sacred elder blessing each and every one of us. It landed on the plate of the woman who desperately needed to know about her father's love. The stillness turned to excitement then turned to joy, and then to absolute awe. The butterfly flew around the room, lighting in front of a man who had just written a story named after butterflies before leaving as miraculously as it had come. There was not a single one of us who at that moment didn't believe that the butterfly was a sign sent from beyond to affirm that love never dies.

SIGNS SENT FROM BEYOND AFFIRM THAT LOVE LIVES ON

There was a woman at one of my presentations who reminded me that I told her in a reading she had more than a year ago that she should look for feathers as a sign that her life's journey would get better and that she was on the right path. She said she had found her feathers, 278 of them in fact, every day over a 90-day period, including one in a video store. She soon realized that they were all heaven sent and she allowed herself to believe in the beauty of life again.

At that same presentation sat a woman who had just lost her young niece to suicide. I told her in a prior reading that she would get a message from her father in the shape of something round and flat, a sign that he was looking after his daughter's niece on the other side. She found that sign as she and his sister were cleaning out her niece's dresser. It was a commemorative coin she had given her niece many years before, tucked safely away in a little box in the top drawer.

"Roland, I was wondering if you could tell me if the signs I have been finding are from my mother who passed away three years ago at Christmas?" asked a woman who attended one of my small group sessions.

"Tell me about them," I replied to her as she began to share her experiences with the 20 of us who gathered there.

"The first one was in a holiday toy catalog I received a year after she died," she began as she gave us the background. "My mother used to tell us a story about when my older brother was a little boy and the toy he wanted more than anything for Christmas. It was called Mr. Machine. I don't ever recall seeing it, but the image of this toy became a legend in my house during the holidays. Apparently, my brother woke up on Christmas morning and looked through every present until he found what he was looking for. The other gifts didn't matter; the only one he had wished for was right there under the tree, testimony to the kind of holiday magic that makes dreams come true. Mom loved telling that story, and I was always curious about the infamous Mr. Machine. I finally saw a picture of that toy in a holiday catalog. Even more amazing, I opened the catalog to the exact page that Mr. Machine was on. Could that have been a sign from my mother?"

I nodded my affirmation as she continued speaking. "The following year, I was just finishing a story I was writing about my mother and the wonderful family vacation we had all taken in Mount Tremblant. I wrote the last lines during a high school class where I teach English. My students were busy taking an exam and filed out of the room quickly when the bell rang. I left the room shortly thereafter, hoping not to be caught up in the throngs of kids who rushed through the halls between classes. There were 1,100 of them in the school. I bumped into one young man as I hurried out. He was wearing a Mount Tremblant t-shirt."

ONCE YOU ASK FOR A SIGN, ONE WILL BE PRESENTED

I told her that she didn't need me to convince her that those were messages from her mother.

You ask for a sign and a sign is presented. They get stronger and stronger until you believe. Keep believing and you'll find signs when you need to.

I myself have received signs from my dear Tullia since she passed in July of 2007. One of the most memorable of these signs occurred when I was driving to an event when I pulled into a busy downtown shopping center in Stamford, Connecticut to pick up something at the local bakery. The hustle and bustle of Christmastime was evident by the joyful sounds of holiday music ringing through the air, the rush of people getting from one place to another, and the usual anxiety that this time of year often brings. As I was driving into the parking lot, situated peacefully between two cars was this humongous turkey. It seemed to be meditating quietly, sitting comfortably, and staring right at me with no intention of moving. It did not raise a feather, nor stood in a defensive stance, but captivated me with its presence.

Like finding a butterfly on a cold and rainy November night in Ireland, seeing a big turkey in downtown Stamford in winter is just as unusual. But that's how signs work. I had been asking Tullia for a sign that she was all right. After all, I spent my life giving messages and signs to everyone else, surely I should receive one myself. That turkey was sent in response to my prayers, to my request that she bequeath me a spiritual sign of hope and forever. You see Tullia loved life and all of God's creatures in it. Turkeys, however, were particular favorites of hers. For years she had been sending a monthly stipend to a New York farm to keep "her" turkey named Acorn off someone's dinner table. Coincidence? I know it was not. Now not only does Tullia's picture grace my meditation area, so does Acorn's.

If you've ever experienced something over and over again in the most unlikely of places, it's most definitely a sign. Like the red balloon I found one day as I was parked along Rte. 6, a busy stretch of highway that went from Connecticut to Rhode Island. As I sat quietly in my car talking to a friend on my cell phone when something beautiful and unexplainable came over me. I felt lightness inside, tingling engulfed me and I looked to my left. There before me was the most magnificent spiritual gift that I had ever received thus far. A red heart shaped helium-filled balloon with the words "I Love You" on it. It was floating horizontally, instead of upward with the wind, along my car, as if someone was walking the balloon. I thought for a moment that my imagination had finally escaped me and I was lost in some far away place. But I looked again, and it was floating along my car, around to the front, up a slight embankment and nudged itself upon one small twig. It swayed in the wind, as if waving to me. I got out and picked up the balloon and took it home with me to keep as a reminder of the loving messages we received every day.

I was so inspired by this experience that I brought it with me to several presentations, for I knew it was a symbol of love sent from beyond. If we just dare to look, each of us can find our red balloon as we move forward on our journey. After sharing that story, I would hear from clients who told me that they too had found their red balloon. It wasn't about the balloon; it was a metaphor about the essence and beauty of love. This is an example of how spiritual communication begins. Once you are open to it, its loving power is never ending.

Months later I was at a retreat when the story of the red balloon came up again. Only this time, I wasn't the one doing the talking. I was doing a reading with a woman at the retreat when her husband's spirit joined our conversation. "Please tell her I love her in a big way," he said. "Give her your red balloon."

I silently fought with him over his request, imploring with him not to take away my balloon. He persisted and I relented. As I handed his wife the red balloon she cried announcing that he would always say I love you in the biggest way this was no surprise to her. She knew in that moment that my stopping at a highway hundreds of miles from her home months before was not by chance, but spirit and her husband orchestrating such an event.

Messages can be subtle or strong. They can come when we least expect them, before a prayer or after a prayer. They come when we need the support or when we the need courage and they always wrap us in unconditional knowing that our voice is heard.

My introduction to Lady Tilly of Sherbrooke during a Reiki session took me by complete surprise. I was working on a client when I heard the sound of a gentle wind blowing in my right ear. It happened several times. Most of which I attempted to ignore, too tired, too busy, or too something to give it credence. But as we know now there is great persistence when messages need to get through. After much time, in the darkness of my healing room, I had a vision of the most beautiful fairy angel I had ever seen. Her wings were made of purple and blue and she was suspended in flight, gently flapping her wings as if she were directing an orchestra of musicians. Behind her a vision of a tree whose branches and limbs had reached out for centuries and centuries before that.

I looked back down at the woman on the massage table and wondered if she too could see this magnificent sight. She was lying on her back with her eyes half open. I wasn't sure if I could share this vision with her. Chances are she would probably think I was a little strange. But somehow the persistence of this beautiful entity caused me to share what I was seeing.

I had chosen my mission of being a conduit for spiritual healing and knew that, however crazy it may sound to the person in front of me, I must share what I hear. I proceeded to describe the fairy angel and the grand old tree in detail to the woman on the table. To my surprise my client uttered no word or exclamation of joy, just deafening silence filled the space. She didn't say a word until her session was complete. Then she turned her back to me, and there, tattooed on her skin, was the fairy angel that I had seen. The woman laughed with acceptance and pulled up her pant leg. To my surprise, there stood the tree, with its great branches, as an anchor for her journey. The last time I had seen this particular client, a month before, she didn't have any tattoos. She told me that it took 100 individual tattoos to create these two pictures.

After she left, I contemplated the sequence of events that lead to the moment of hearing the wind gently blowing in my ear to the moment she revealed exactly what I had seen. I was, again, in awe of the spiritual beauty that is in every second of time. I prayed for a message and what I heard was exactly what I needed.

We are not to forget who we are. We are not what others say we are. We are who we have chosen to be. We are symbols of light. We have wings, even when others cannot see them. We must know it first. We must believe it first. Be guided by your own wings.

Moments like these are truly life changing. They happen more frequently than you can imagine and they define who we are. If we ignore them, we are unable to take ourselves to the next level.

There are no coincidences. All of these stories are synchronicities that are a part of a much bigger picture, a picture that involves all aspects of living, of being, of believing and of loving who we truly are. There are moments in which you feel like giving up and something happens to lift your spirits and renew your faith. That, my friends, is the mystery that makes life full of endless possibilities. That is what my story and your journey are all about. But as awe-inspiring as each of our journeys is, there is so much more to the story in a place called heaven.

My part in all of this? I am here to simply pass along the messages that heaven exists, within us and around us. It is in every smile and in every rose, in every sunset and in every embrace. It is above and beyond the clouds and deeply rooted within in a place where the soul meets the heart. It is everything, and everyone and every moment. It is every breath. It is in hello and goodbye, and thank you and I love you. Heaven is all that we are and all that we become.

Did you ever hear the story of the little sparrow that was found one day lying in a dusty road with his tiny little feet in the air?

"What are you doing in the middle of the road, you wimpy little bird?" asked a horseman who came upon the tiny creature lying in his way.

"I heard that heaven was falling," said the little bird "and I am trying to help hold it up."

"You think your puny little legs can hold up heaven?" the horseman laughed.

"One does what one can," the little bird replied.

I know more than ever that the journey of my life has been my teacher. The words, stories, and messages, I have heard from heaven is my divine purpose. Every sacrifice, every gift, every obstacle, every lesson has given me the absolute freedom to be who I am.

I have felt the breath of God. I have heard the angels sing. I have seen the light from those I meet here and those that have passed on. I know that all this sits in a place of reality...if we have the courage to believe it.

I have climbed my own mountain of understanding, and I know, like you, we all have a mission, a purpose and a place. This is mine.

Like the little sparrow who intends to do what he can, I will continue to hold the knowing, the energy and the gift that there is no death. Death is a step beyond and into a place called Heaven.

And then there was heaven...above, beyond and within me.

CPSIA information can be obtained at www.ICGtesting.com
Printed in the USA
BVOW061521060312

284515BV00001B/1/P

9 780982 453605